Bobby Fischer Comes Home

Helgi Olafsson

Bobby Fischer Comes Home

The final years in Iceland

A saga of friendship and lost illusions

New In Chess 2012

© 2012 New In Chess
Published by New In Chess, Alkmaar, The Netherlands
www.newinchess.com

Cover design: Volken Beck
Cover: Summer 2005, Bobby Fischer walks down the Almannagja rift in
Thingvellir, Iceland. Photo: Einar Einarsson
Editors: Dirk Jan ten Geuzendam, Sarah Hurst
Production: Joop de Groot
ISBN: 978-90-5691-381-6

Contents

A happy part of his life

Bobby Fischer was the reason why many many people took up chess in the 70s. There's a whole generation of people who still remember the match in Reykjavik in 1972 and the impact it had. Of course, I've also grown up with the Bobby Fischer legend and I included several of his openings in my repertoire. His influence was huge.

I had not really imagined meeting him in Iceland when I went there in March 2006 for the Glitnir Blitz tournament. Therefore it's difficult to compare what I expected with what eventually happened. One day Helgi asked me if I wanted to meet Bobby and I was of course delighted to do so. It was kind of surreal because you finally meet this legend who lives a reclusive life and is difficult to get close to. But when we met we ended up doing some very mundane stuff. I showed him some games from the recent Wijk aan Zee tournament and he analysed them on his pocket set. This was an experience I hadn't had in a while, because nowadays we tend to do everything on computers. I could see that Bobby in a way was still frozen in time, from his way of analysing, his conclusions. Many things struck me that revealed that he was still very much into the game, but he hadn't really kept track of recent developments.

Reykjavik came at the end of a very troubled period in Bobby's life. The 90s were very difficult for him and when he finally got to Iceland I was relieved as well, even before meeting him. I felt that he'd be happy there and in fact that's how I felt our encounter to be, that Bobby had finally found a place where he could be at peace. The Icelanders treated him with respect for who he was, but at the same time knew to leave him alone to enjoy his life there. He could endlessly wander the streets of Reykjavik, left to himself. It was a bit surprising to find that Bobby was also getting onto buses and exploring Reykjavik, mentally making a list of restaurants and shops that he wanted to visit later. He told me that he had still not found many good Indian restaurants and Indian shops. We spoke a bit about that and he asked me about some Indian products, one for headaches and things like that. As said, I could not have imagined meeting him, but if I had I doubt that I could have imagined such a conversation!

Then he asked me a bit about chess. He felt that chess had become much too computerized and there was very little scope for creativity left. He seemed disillusioned about modern chess, but maybe that's a typical thing for old chess players. There comes a certain point when they feel it's changing too fast.

The main feeling I got was that he was really happy in Iceland and our meeting was enjoyable for that reason. I also think he really trusted Helgi. He was the only person through whom you could reach Bobby and Helgi did a lot to make Bobby happy in Iceland. Bobby really needed someone to rescue him at that point. Therefore I am glad that Helgi decided to write this book and I hope the reader will enjoy the stories about his experiences with Bobby, about what was a happy part of his life.

Viswanathan Anand
Chennai, March 2012

Chapter One

In regard to the date of the introduction of the game into Iceland it is undeniable
that the country's most distinguished son, Snorri Sturluson, was more or less
acquainted with the game, when he narrated, in St. Olaf's saga, the story of King
Canute the Great and his retainer, Jarl Ulf the rich.
Willard Fiske, *Chess in Iceland*

The first time I heard the name Bobby Fischer was in the summer of 1968. I was 11 years old. In June I had moved with my family from Reykjavik to the Westman Islands off the south coast of Iceland. My father had taken a post there as the local bank manager.

The islands are said to have been named after a few Irish slaves who were tracked down by the man who discovered Iceland, Ingolfur Arnarson. His blood brother, Hjörleifur, had been killed by his Irish slaves and the ensuing manhunt ended in the Westman islands. The exact history of the name is shrouded in mystery. Some scholars have suggested that Westman applied to all the people living west of Iceland, that is the Irish, Scots and Picts.

Heimaey is the only island that is populated in the Westman Islands archipelago. The most dramatic, tragic and significant episode in the history of Heimaey took place in June 1627, a tragedy which in Iceland is referred to as the Turkish abductions. Pirates from Algiers sailed to the Westman Islands in 15 vessels. The main harbour was well guarded but the pirates went ashore at a creek which is now called Pirates' Cove. They captured or killed several hundred people, and the young and healthy were sold into slavery on the Barbary Coast in North Africa.

At the time my family arrived there in the spring of 1968, around 5,000 people were living in the Westman Islands. What sticks in my memory from my first days and weeks was the great anticipation for an upcoming event: water was finally coming to Heimaey. The huge undertaking of laying an undersea water pipeline from the mainland signalled the end of all the homemade rain collectors.

One day in June I went to the house of a newfound friend, Tomas. For some months I had been under the spell of a new hobby, chess, and I tried to persuade him to accompany me to a special event: Soviet grandmaster Evgeny Vasiukov had been flown in by helicopter. I had noticed a poster in a window of the town hall saying: The famous Soviet grandmaster Evgeny

Vasiukov, winner of the Reykjavik international chess tournament, will give a simultaneous exhibition Saturday at 2 pm. Everybody is welcome. Be there.

We were discussing the prospects of going to the simul when my friend's father, Johannes, stepped in and encouraged us, saying with a smile: 'One day you might play Fischer or Petrosian!' At the time I was familiar with the names of some Soviet grandmasters, but I had never heard the name Bobby Fischer before.

As the poster read, Vasiukov had just won the 3rd Reykjavik international tournament dedicated to the memory of the chess writer, publisher and philanthropist Daniel Willard Fiske, an American who authored the book *Chess in Iceland and in Icelandic Literature*. Fiske was an ardent lover both of chess and Iceland. As a young man he compiled the tournament book of the first American Chess Congress in 1857, the first great triumph of his friend Paul Morphy. Later, as professor of North European languages at Cornell University, he collected an Icelandic library of 10,000 volumes. After his death in 1904 he bequeathed his chess books to the National Library in Reykjavik.

In spite of spirited efforts by the local chess club, the simul was not very well attended. Just over twenty players participated and I expected it to be a rout. I seem to remember that three players managed to make a draw, largely due to the leniency of the grandmaster, but some of his opponents did not seem to have much knowledge of the game. Even though I was not playing I took up the role of an active observer. When one of the players was surprised by a pawn capture I proudly explained the *en passant* rule to him.

I spent the rest of the summer playing football, but in the autumn I joined the Westman Islands chess club. The club had a fine location on the second floor of a house called Drifandi, which, roughly translated, means House of Energy. With their wooden floors the spacious rooms were a very suitable venue. There were some other activities in there, too – one night a documentary film made by Pall Steingrimsson was shown in an adjacent room. There was a lot of laughter at the beginning of it when Pall appeared on screen as the MGM lion.

I met several youngsters at the club, but to my surprise it seemed to me that chesswise I held some advantage over most of them – maybe because I had already read a chess book by Pyotr Romanovsky featuring the games of the great 19th-century masters. I also played with my father, a decent player, almost every day.

The Westman Islands Championship in December 1968 was an important gathering. The tournament was divided into three categories and I was put into second category. I had great respect for all the adult players and even made a habit of writing down entire games of importance as they were played.

Two of the oldest players, Gustaf Finnbogason and Sigurberg Bogason, had such an aura of dignity as they played their moves that from then on I took it for granted that chess was indeed a royal game. Later I heard they were actually rather weak players, but that was not what it was about for me. I felt attracted by the atmosphere and the rituals. Of the regulars at the club almost everyone seemed to have a certain typicality. One player, when given the chance, consistently employed the French Defence, another opened only with the English Opening, and a third answered the king's pawn with the Scandinavian Defence. Then there was a player who was generally considered to be a great scholar. He had read many chess books and because of that an aura of higher knowledge surrounded him. But he rarely played. He reminded me of a person my father had told me about who was sometimes seen on the streets of Reykjavik carrying the German edition of Alekhine's book *On the Road to the World Championship* under his arm.

When the chess season in the spring of 1969 ended the chess club was moved to another location. By then I had subscribed to the only Icelandic chess magazine. In one of the first issues I received there was an article about Bobby Fischer and a tournament in Vinkovci in Yugoslavia. Every Fischer game from the tournament was published with light notes and I played through them religiously.

In the summer of 1969 I played over every game of the World Championship match between Boris Spassky and Tigran Petrosian, which ended in a victory for the challenger and made Spassky the tenth World Champion in chess history. In the autumn I followed with great interest a tournament in Palma de Mallorca won by Bent Larsen. In the early rounds the Dane lost a game against the World Champion. In an ending in which he was a pawn up, Larsen fell into a trap and was defeated by Spassky, who nonetheless had a rather lacklustre performance.

Around that time, Freysteinn Thorbergsson, one of Iceland's best players and a former Nordic champion, paid the Westman Islands chess club a visit. A clock simul was staged and I participated. We played a Queen's Gambit and for a long time he had a winning position, but I managed to put up a stubborn defence and tricked him in the complications. After 44 moves I offered Freysteinn a draw, which he accepted. When the game was finished he asked me how old I was. I said that I had just turned thirteen.

From then on chess was becoming ever more important to me, but chess books and magazines were scarce. The next big event to look forward to was the Reykjavik international tournament at the beginning of 1970. It was won by the new Icelandic chess star Gudmundur Sigurjonsson, who was seen as a great promise. Of crucial importance was his game with Fridrik Olafsson, Iceland's first ever grandmaster and a living legend in our country. Gudmundur won after a complicated fight.

Personally, I had set my sights on the Icelandic Junior Championship in 1970, which was to be held in Reykjavik. I felt eager and ambitious. Traditionally it took place during Easter. For a moment the unpredictable Icelandic weather threatened to throw a spanner in the works. At the time when the tournament was about to start a heavy storm hit the Westman Islands. When I was about to board the ferry the conditions were so bad that the captain advised against my sailing to Reykjavik. He didn't think it was a good idea for a kid travelling alone. The following day the storm had subsided and I took a flight to the capital. The opposition wasn't hard to overcome and I won with a clean score, 12 out of 12.

The next day I was walking the streets of Reykjavik with my cousin Thorir, who bought a copy of the newspaper *Visir*. There on the front page I read: '13-year-old Westman Islander defeats everybody.' I was not that impressed, but when I returned to school the kids gave me strange looks, staring at me as if I was something special.

At the time another chess event was much written about in the papers. A match on 10 boards between the Soviet Union and a Rest of the World team in Belgrade had brought together all the best chess players in the world. There had been a lot of speculation about who would play World Champion Boris Spassky on Board 1: Bent Larsen, who had some spectacular recent results to show for himself, or Bobby Fischer, who had not played for a while. To the surprise of many Fischer had agreed to play on second board.

I was walking to school one morning when a schoolmate of mine told me that Spassky had beaten Larsen in only 17 moves. Spassky had to be a true world champion, I thought. Then the newspaper *Morgunbladid* also published a beautiful win by Fischer over Petrosian, whom I still regarded as my favourite player. I liked Petrosian because he had been World Champion and because of the depth of his game. Looking at his picture before he started to play Spassky he struck me as very dignified person. Fischer's win against Petrosian was an inspiring event for a young chess player. How could it be that the American defeated the ultra-solid Russian so convincingly?

In the summer of 1970 my parents, as was an accepted custom, decided to send me to work at a farm in Hunavatnssysla in northern Iceland. Volcano Hekla had been sleeping since 1947, but had erupted in May and the ashes were scattered all over the country. The farmer at Öxl where I lived and worked encountered considerable hardship, but he never complained. His pride were his horses, but he had sold the one he loved the most to a German buyer.

The well-known chess player Jonas Halldorsson, who was in his early thirties, lived in the area, at a farm called Leysingjastadir. I visited him quite frequently and each time we played more than twenty blitz games. He was far stronger than me, but I still won a few games from him. I once asked him: 'Why do you never play the Sicilian Defence against me?' and he answered: 'That I would only do against Palmi from Akri.' Palmi was a farmer he knew. In the summer of 1973 I heard the tragic news that Jonas had drowned in Lake Hopid.

This district was at the time still in what could be called semi-isolation. The 'country telephone' was a strange form of communication. People had to be careful with their spoken words, as it was possible for others to pick up the phones in nearby farmhouses and listen to the conversations. Each farm had its own ring tone. Once a week a beaten-down bus arrived from Reykjavik bringing – among many other essentials – the newspapers. I read in *Morgunbladid* that Bobby Fischer was leading a chess tournament in Buenos Aires with a score of 10½ points out of 11. It was only later that I realized that around this time he was becoming my chess hero.

In September there were reports of thousands of people flocking to Siegen, West Germany, where the biennial Chess Olympiad was being held, to see the much-awaited encounter between Spassky and Fischer in the match between the Soviet Union and the USA. This was probably the most important chess game of 1970. Spassky won a tense struggle. But this setback for Fischer was followed by the Palma Interzonal, where the American scored another incredible victory. After 23 rounds Fischer finished 3½ points ahead of Larsen, Geller and Hübner.

At the beginning of 1971 Icelanders turned their attention to the small town of Wijk aan Zee in the Netherlands, where Fridrik Olafsson was playing. Fridrik took an early lead and was especially forceful against the young stars, winning a beautiful game against Robert Hübner. Then he met Ulf Andersson – a fascinating game in all its aspects. It was adjourned four times, with Fridrik finally winning in 105 moves after 13 hours of play.

In the spring Icelandic TV had a chess programme. Bent Larsen came to Iceland and played a televised match against Fridrik. The time limit was 30 minutes each for the completion of every game, which was quite unusual in those days. Bent won with a score of 3½-2½.

The Candidates' matches of 1971, which were going to determine who was to challenge World Champion Boris Spassky in 1972, shocked the chess world. In the second half of May Bobby Fischer baffled friend and foe by defeating Mark Taimanov with a score of 6-0 in Vancouver. Fischer's next opponent in the knock-out schedule that was leading up to the World Championship match, was Bent Larsen. Before that match, which was played in Denver, I heard a radio interview with Fridrik Olafsson, who was usually a very reserved individual. Fridrik had earned his grandmaster title at the Interzonal tournament in Portoroz in 1958 by sharing fifth place with the 15-year-old Bobby Fischer. From Fridrik's excited voice I realized that Bobby Fischer was transcending chess. 'Bent Larsen will fight Bobby Fischer with great determination. It will be no walkover', he said. His expectations didn't come true. Bobby again won 6-0. Afterwards Larsen complained about the stifling heat in Denver. From a chess technical point of view it could be argued that he didn't have a decent defence against Bobby's king's pawn openings, and as White he never really got anything out of the openings.

Now everybody was eagerly awaiting the Fischer-Petrosian match, the Candidates' Final that would produce the challenger to Boris Spassky. That match started in the Argentinian capital Buenos Aires in September. I was walking down Vestmannabraut Street when the chairman of the chess club, Arnar Sigurmundsson, saw me through a window of his office and called me in. 'Fischer won the first game', he said, and he was all smiles. But the following day my mother brought me different news. 'Do you know what happened?' she said, and without awaiting my guess added, 'Petrosian won.'

This loss in the second game was the end of an unparalleled winning streak in chess history. Fischer had won his last seven games in Palma de Mallorca without even allowing a single draw. Combined with the two 6-0 routs against Taimanov and Larsen, and the first game against Petrosian, this added up to 20 wins in a row against grandmasterly opposition.

The match against Petrosian continued with three draws. In Game 6 Fischer won a long ending as Black and thus destroyed Petrosian's fighting spirit. Having broken his opponent's resistance Fischer was now unstoppable. He concluded with three more wins to clinch the match 6½-2½.

A few weeks later there were reports in our national press of discussions within the Icelandic Chess Federation about making a bid for the upcoming World Championship match. All of FIDE's national federations were allowed to do so. In February 1972, when it had not yet been decided where the match would take place, Bobby Fischer came to Iceland together with Ed Edmondson, the Executive Director of the U.S. Chess Federation. When I saw him on television, Edmondson struck me as a very dignified and responsible man who cared a great deal about his star player. Bobby stayed at the Hotel Saga and gave a press conference in his hotel room. There he kept saying that it was up to FIDE to choose a venue for the match, but later we learned that his preferred location was Belgrade. Fischer was quite handsome and well dressed, but seemed a little shy. From the photographs published in the newspapers I concluded that he carried chess magazines under his arm wherever he went.

By coincidence the 5th Reykjavik international chess tournament began the same weekend Bobby Fischer was in town. He agreed to honour the tournament by going there together with Gudmundur Thorarinsson, the President of the Icelandic Chess Federation, and Ed Edmondson. Among the 16 participants were Leonid Stein, a Soviet grandmaster and winner of the recently-held Alekhine Memorial tournament in Moscow, Vlastimil Hort from Czechoslovakia, Ulf Andersson from Sweden, Jan Timman from the Netherlands, the Romanian Florin Gheorghiu, the young Soviet grandmaster Vladimir Tukmakov, the best English player Raymond Keene, and the Icelandic stars Fridrik Olafsson and Gudmundur Sigurjonsson.

When Fischer appeared in the tournament hall the spectators slowly, almost hesitantly, moved in his direction, as if drawn by a magnet. They were both curious and admiring. The room was dimly lit, but Fischer was standing there by a pole like a Greek god, engrossed in a game between Raymond Keene and Leonid Stein. In a sharp game Keene had obtained a promising position which Fischer assessed as winning for White. As the newspapers reported, he told Gudmundur, 'Stein is dead lost.' Shortly afterwards a young boy working the demonstration boards put up a sign in Icelandic. 'Did Stein resign?' Bobby asked. 'No, they agreed a draw', Gudmundur answered. By then Bobby Fischer had had enough of this tournament and left.

The English International Master later admitted that he gave away the draw too quickly. Even today's chess computers fail to prove a forced win for Keene from the final position, but he could and should have continued playing. There was no risk involved. At the time a draw with a Soviet grandmaster with either colour was considered a success. It took a player from a new generation to challenge this generally-held view, and later that young man called Tony Miles easily surpassed Raymond Keene and the other English chess players.

In Amsterdam the bids for the World Championship match were opened. Apparently there was a deadlock between Reykjavik, Spassky's first choice, and Belgrade, Fischer's first choice. The only satisfactory solution, by the admission of FIDE President Max Euwe, was to split the match between the two cities. The first leg would be held in Belgrade, the second leg in Reykjavik. Because of Fischer's 6-0 wins over Larsen and Taimanov, I worried that only one game would be played in Iceland. Then the Yugoslavs all of a sudden terminated all negotiations. Edmondson was fired from Fischer's camp. Fischer's deadline for committing to play almost expired. Was he going amok?

At this point, without any hesitation, the Icelandic Chess Federation, backed by the Icelandic government, seized the opportunity and agreed to stage the whole match. The summer held great promise.

Chapter Two

Thereupon I sit in the great hall and see those tiny men in the distance fencing and armed with knowledge, logic, inventiveness and rationally restricted daring and whatever other weapons they have.
Thor Vilhjalmsson, writer. From an article published in the Fischer-Spassky match bulletin *Skak* in 1972.

Boris Spassky arrived in Iceland on June 21 during the period when the sun never sets. By coming to Iceland two weeks before the start of the event he wanted to acclimatize and prepare mentally for the fight ahead. At the airport he was greeted by the president of the Icelandic Chess Federation, Gudmundur Thorarinsson, and his two young daughters, who handed the World Champion a bouquet of flowers. Television was there and Spassky was all smiles and answered most of the questions sincerely. His natural charm won many hearts. He was accompanied by Efim Geller, Nikolai Krogius and Ivo Nei. The presence of a television camera sounds most normal from our present perspective, but actually in 1972 this was still very special in Iceland. RUV, the Icelandic National Broadcasting Service, had transmissions six days a week. No television was broadcast on Thursdays and, till RUV lost its monopoly in 1983, there were no broadcasts in the month of July. So Spassky arrived just in time!

The World Champion and his team checked in at the best hotel in Iceland, the Hotel Saga, with Spassky occupying the presidential suite. Outside his hotel room he had a view over a tennis court that had been built specially for him. Tennis was a sport not played at all in Iceland. Spassky could be seen playing this game with his seconds for many hours in the evenings. Kids kept coming to watch him play and they would sometimes run after the ball, and Spassky would always be very thankful for any such favour.

Spassky would take long walks, especially in that western part of Reykjavik by the seashore. He even attended a soccer match between Iceland and Denmark, won by Denmark 5-2, at a stadium very close to Laugardalshöll, the venue of the World Championship match. He also went fishing in a river in Grimsa which runs through the south-west part of Iceland, less than 100 kilometres from the capital.

I wondered why Spassky had played so little before the match. After a splendid performance in 1970, when he swept the field at the IBM tournament in Amsterdam and scored an impressive 9½ points from 12 games at the Siegen Olympiad, all he could show were some meagre results in three tournaments in 1971. He came joint first in the Canadian Open in Vancouver, took 2nd place in Gothenburg behind the young star Ulf Andersson, and finished 6th to 7th place with Tal at the Alekhine Memorial at the end of 1971. His best result came in a team tournament where he scored 3½ points out of 4.

Compared to Fischer's dazzling performance in the Interzonal tournament and the Candidates' matches, it was not worthy of a world champion. But then someone pointed out that since his first Candidates' match in 1965, Spassky had played eight matches, convincingly winning seven. Besides, people were happy to have Spassky in Reykjavik. He didn't at all typify the 'Soviet' person, but seemed more like a free-spirited individual whose status had allowed him to dwell well above the rest of the pack.

With Spassky in Reykjavik, the public's attention turned to the challenger. A series of photographs appeared in the newspapers of Fischer working out in a gym at Grossinger's in upstate New York, the legendary resort hotel, where the great heavyweight champions of the world would train, such as Rocky Marciano and Joe Louis. He had not yet hired an official second, but finally he asked his childhood friend and grandmaster Bill Lombardy to accompany him to Reykjavik.

Fischer was expected to land in Reykjavik early in the morning of June 29. The first game was scheduled to be played on July 2 at 5 pm. The beautifully hand-carved Staunton Jaques pieces had been set up in Laugardalshöll. There was a chessboard made from Icelandic rock with greenish dark squares, but the organizers also had several wooden boards in stock.

The idea of the table itself was taken from the ones the organizers of the Havana Chess Olympiad in 1966 had made. The novelty there was that the players could rest their arms on a neatly-cut leather cushion. Fridrik Olafsson had one at his home, as Fidel Castro had made sure that all first board players of the participating countries got such a table as a present and lasting souvenir.

By now the prospects of the 'Match of the Century' taking place were looking grim. Fischer was indeed driven to JFK airport on July 28, but he failed to board the plane. On seeing the flocks of reporters at the airport he ran away. The photographs published in the newspapers the following morning depicted a confused individual desperate to flee from the paparazzi chasing him.

The opening ceremony, however, went on as planned on the evening of Saturday, July 1, at the National Theatre. The President of Iceland, Kristjan Eldjarn, was there, as well as Soviet Ambassador Sergei Astavin, U.S. Ambassador Theodor Tremblay, the Mayor of Reykjavik, Geir Hallgrimsson, FIDE President Max Euwe and many more dignitaries. Bobby Fischer's seat was empty.

The following day Max Euwe postponed the first game on the grounds that the challenger was ill, and said that it would be played on July 4. Later, in a letter of apology, the Dutch former World Champion would acknowledge that with his decision he violated the match agreement and thus broke FIDE laws.

Fischer's team, already in Iceland, had been engaged in heated debates about countless minor details, but the real problem was that they sorely lacked a mandate. Their signature did not mean a thing and Fischer had categorically refused to sign any document pushed towards him. The saviour of the match from this paralysing stalemate all of a sudden appeared early Monday morning. A British businessman by the name of Jim Slater not only offered to double the prize-fund, but also put forward a proposition Bobby could not resist: if money is a problem, here it is. So come out, chicken, and play. By then U.S. Secretary of State Henry Kissinger had urged Fischer in a telephone call '... to go to Reykjavik and beat the Russians', as he put it.

In the early hours on Independence Day, July 4, 1972, Bobby Fischer landed in Iceland. He ignored the media circus that had been waiting for him for days. One reporter was heard saying after the American had rushed past him and his colleagues: 'We may have been unable to get a word out of this guy, but at least I don't need to get here every goddamn morning anymore.'

As Fischer was moving fast past the throngs of onlookers, mostly members of the press, ICF President Gudmundur Thorarinsson jumped in his way and almost forced him to shake hands. Then Fischer took a seat in a waiting taxi, slamming the door. He had demanded a police escort from the airport, a 50-kilometre drive from Keflavik to the house where he was supposed to live during the match. A major obstacle had been removed. Fischer was in Iceland.

At noon that day I picked up the tabloid paper, *Visir*. There he was: the great Bobby Fischer. It showed a photograph of a dishevelled and jet-lagged Fischer standing in front of his house, wearing a T-shirt, and he was quoted posing a question to a policeman who had been sent there to safeguard the area: 'Hey dude, where's my luggage?'

The drawing of lots was supposed to take place at noon in the Hotel Esja close to the playing hall, with the first match game starting at 5 pm the same day. I somehow could not see that happening. It was all summed up on the front page of one major American newspaper: 'Spassky's move: He walks out.'

By the time the drawing of lots was due to take at noon on July 4, Bobby was fast asleep. He had sent Bill Lombardy to represent him. When Lombardy arrived together with the rest of Bobby's delegation, Efim Geller issued a statement condemning Bobby's behaviour and then stormed out of the Hotel Esja as Nikita Krushchev had done at the 1960 Paris summit when President Eisenhower refused to apologize for the U-2 spy aircraft that had been shot down above Soviet soil. After a letter of apology from Bobby the storm subsided for a while and the drawing of lots took place on July 7. On stage Spassky hid two pawns behind his back in the palms of his hands and Fischer drew Black.

I very much wanted to be in the Laugardalshöll arena when the match started, but in the Westman Islands you were supposed to go to work immediately after school had finished. So I took up a job at the freezing plant Fiskidjan, spending most of the time chatting with and carrying fresh fish to the ladies working at the tables.

Finally, on Tuesday, July 11 at exactly 5 pm, chief arbiter Lothar Schmid pressed the clock of the World Champion, who responded by playing the move that had netted him a full point in his last two encounters with Fischer, 1.d4. For seven minutes of the game Fischer's chair, flown in from New York, and an exact copy of the one he sat in during his match against Petrosian in Buenos Aires, was empty. Then he emerged from behind the curtains to a thunderous ovation from the audience in the packed playing hall.

The match had been building in volume, but now what about the first game? It looked like another Petrosian match. Nothing much was happening and then, suddenly, all hell broke loose. Fischer captured a poisoned pawn on h2. He believed he could get away with this shocking capture, but there was a gap in his calculations and after the game had been adjourned the World Champion took the full point in the second session.

Meanwhile Fischer's tireless search for new enemies continued. Now his rage was aimed at the Icelandic film crew. They were filming the match for Chester Fox, who had obtained the filming and photography rights in the playing hall. Fischer didn't turn up for the second game, and forfeited it. It seemed that the match would soon be over and there were reports of Fischer booking several flights back home or even to Greenland.

Still, the third game took place on schedule, on Sunday, July 16. By agreeing to play the game in a closed room, Boris Spassky saved the match and the legacy of Bobby Fischer. This moment in chess history seems to have stayed with Spassky as a deep wound in his psyche, as became clear to me many years later.

In late September 2004, Iceland played a match on four boards with France in the French parliament in Paris. Afterwards there was a knockout tournament with all the 16 participants competing. It was part of an Icelandic festival in France. Spassky was there as a guest of honour. On a Saturday evening the Icelandic players had dinner with Boris and his wife Marina. Bobby Fischer's plight was on everyone's mind, as at that moment he was being held in a detention centre in Japan after his arrest at Tokyo airport. All of a sudden Spassky turned to me and asked very directly: 'Helgi, if I had chosen to stay in the rest room during my match with Bobby, what do you think he would have done?'

His question was both sincere and straightforward and required an honest answer: 'I think Bobby was always trying to impose his will upon you. I am sure it would have made him furious', I answered.

Spassky was quiet for a while and I don't know what went through his mind. He could have terminated the match by leaving the playing arena that day.

I finally came to Reykjavik for the ninth game. By then Fischer had built a commanding lead by winning four games. Entering the hall for the first time, the most noticeable feature I saw was the enormous demonstration board the organizers had brought from Belgrade. It was possibly part of a deal with the Yugoslav partner when the match was planned to be split between Reykjavik and Belgrade. The demonstration board had been built specially for the Soviet Union vs. The Rest of the World match in 1970. It was placed in the centre and added to the grand setting in Laugardalshöll. A fine piece of equipment, it had no sensor features: three young Icelandic chess players, Benedikt Jonasson, Kristjan Gudmundsson and Ögmundur Kristinsson, relayed the moves as quickly as possible.

I really enjoyed being in the big hall, but for me the main action was in the press room. My cousin Thorir Olafsson, a strong local player who had been living in Colombia, was writing chess columns for a Colombian newspaper. In this capacity he had access to the press room and he brought me there together with his oldest son. We would sometimes guess what opening would be played, and I remember how surprised he was when I rightly predicted the opening of the thirteenth game, Alekhine's Defence, an opening Fischer had played on four occasions in 1970.

In the press room lively and knowledgeable discussions took place. American grandmaster Robert Byrne had just started to write for *The New York Times*, and he was sitting quietly in a corner with his typewriter. Another ever-present person was the former Danish champion Jens Enevoldsen. His compatriot Bent Larsen visited Iceland at the beginning of the match and at least once afterwards when Fischer already had a commanding lead. He gave a few interviews expressing his opinion that his loss to Fischer in the summer of 1971 didn't mean a thing and repeating that the extreme weather conditions in Denver had made it impossible for him to play. He commented on the games in front of a huge audience and once in a while he popped up in the press room when I was there.

A newly-arrived Lubomir Kavalek and Larsen discussed the thirteenth game after the adjournment, a game with many almost surreal positions. I think I have a fairly good overview when it comes to games from World Championship matches, and not a single game equals the complications in that one. Even though I was a complete nobody I remember how respectful these two grandmasters were towards some of my suggestions. On the 64th move Fischer could give up one of his passed pawns in order to let his king invade the white position. This move was not high on Kavalek and Larsen's priority list, most probably because they knew that Bobby by nature was reluctant to give up material. I was rooting for this move before it was played, but the idea was politely rejected. In the end, thanks to this move, Fischer won.

Another prominent figure who sometimes wandered into the press room was Bobby's official second, William Lombardy. In 1957, Lombardy had been the first American to win the World Junior Championship and he even did so with a perfect score, 11 points from 11 games. In 1960 he played first board for the U.S. at the World Student Team Championship in Leningrad. The U.S. won and Lombardy won the gold medal on first board, one of his victims being Boris Spassky. Instead of a chess career he pursued a career in the Catholic Church and in 1967 he was ordained a priest. Later he left the church, but in Reykjavik he was still a priest, even if he didn't dress like one. He was friendly, though he sometimes made slightly sarcastic remarks. Ingi R. Johannsson was the best Icelandic chess player frequenting the room, and I sensed well his deep understanding of the game.

Before games large groups of people would wait for Boris and Bobby to emerge from their cars backstage at the playing hall. I usually joined in and because of all the excitement it was a lot of fun.

After Fischer won the thirteenth game there was never any doubt really about the outcome of the match. Game after game, Spassky pressed hard but Fischer defended his three-point lead with complete sang froid. He now curiously adopted a new tactic, never employing the same line twice. On September 1, 1972 Boris Spassky phoned in his resignation of the adjourned twenty-first game and Robert James Fischer became the 11th World Chess Campion. The final score was 12½-8½.

Chapter Three

The island of Iceland is an anomaly and a marvel – an anomaly in its natural
history, for almost everywhere in its domain we find the living fierceness of
volcanic heat coping with the death-like desolation of Arctic cold...
Chess in Iceland – Willard Fiske

The match was coming to a close in August. Bobby Fischer stayed on for another three weeks, but in the end everyone left. The players and their entourage, the press, chess tourists, the entire circus had gone. The stories remained and became part of chess history. An opening ceremony without a challenger, the KGB and the CIA, two dead flies found in a chair in a search for secret electronic equipment, Fischer's friendship with Icelandic policeman, carpenter and dancer Saemi Rokk, his solitary walks in the fog, Spassky's dance with a brunette from Borgarnes, Fischer bowling at the U.S. base at Keflavik, endless disputes and worldwide headlines.

I gave the match's meaning a lot of thought. Bobby Fischer would surely win, but where would he play next? Would the World Championship title make him happy? Why didn't he get married? Why did he live in hotels? Was playing chess a worthy occupation?

One day in mid-August during the match two girls flew to Reykjavik from the Westman Islands, and in the middle of the day the three of us decided to see a film together in a small theatre called Hafnarbio, an old barrack erected by the British troops during the occupation of Iceland in the Second World War. *A Man Called Horse* was delightful entertainment, with the main character, played by Richard Harris, being captured by Native Americans.

I sat between these two beautiful 15-year-old girls and the one who was slightly older whispered in my ear: 'Helgi. Do you think Indians can grow a beard?' And I answered: 'I don't know.' When the film was over the three of us walked down nearby Skulagata Street, heading to the city centre. Several cars passed by and some of the drivers honked their horns. The girls started to laugh and I just smiled.

Once back in the Westman islands I kept on working at the Fiskidjan freezing plant. During busy times, and they were numerous in Heimaey, it was almost impossible to get the smell of fish out of your nose. When I approached the main building situated just a few hundred metres away from my home, the smell would hit me midway. I liked the people at Fiskidjan, particularly the women who had worked there for many years. My job was to carry fish to a few tables scattered among nearly 30 tables in total on the enormous ground floor of the plant. Some of the women started their working day at noon. Occasionally an old man would come to their table and sharpen their knives without uttering a single word. Loud music was played all day long. For the foreign visitors who occasionally came to watch the workplace in action, it was probably easy to assume that it was not at all normal for teenagers, or even 12-year-old kids, to work long hours here. In fact it was an extremely enjoyable and rewarding experience.

At the chess club no one could offer me any serious opposition. I was simply too strong a player for everybody else on the island and it was clear that my further development was being hampered by lack of competition. Before the Fischer-Spassky match I had sent in two mail orders, for Fischer's *My 60 Memorable Games* and for a collection of his complete games. I didn't know at the time that the latter book was published without Bobby's consent, an outright exploitation of his work. I played through each and every of his games more than once. The harmony in Fischer's play was marvellous, although I probably didn't fully grasp yet how technically strong he was.

There were other distractions. Three young teachers, barely 20 years old, had moved to the Westman Islands and when I got to know them it seemed they represented something new. Meeting them was like catching a breath of fresh air. However, the community seemed to receive them with some scepticism. One day when I was walking near the harbour with a friend we decided to pay a visit to our female history teacher. We were looking for a cat, which our biology teacher wanted to use for one of his lessons. When she answered the door and listened to us on her doorstep she sort of ignored our questions concerning her cat, but when she invited us to come in we found her simply a wonderful creature. She was living in a very old house. I could see no walls as she had hung up shawls made of silk with candles casting light on the beaded curtains. 'These are all the doors in the house', she said with a mysterious smile. The incense she was burning gave the house a typical aroma. She poured us tea with lemon, adding brown sugar. In the background the Cat Stevens album *Catch Bull at Four* was playing. For the next few days his songs kept spinning in my head: *A gardener's daughter stopped me on my way, on the day I was to wed. It is you who I wish to share my body with she said.*

I had a game in the Westman Islands Championship in the evening and was more than twenty minutes late. Arnar Sigurmundsson came up to me

25

and said: 'Helgi, you know Fischer was only seven minutes late.' I promised myself I would never be late for a game of chess again.

After nine rounds I had won all my games in the championship. On January 22, 1973, my 10th round game with Andri Hrolfsson was adjourned in a winning position for me. I walked home alone along Vestmannabraut late at night. Not one of the usual creeps was on the sidewalk calling out 'Fischer', or 'e2-e4', or 'check and mate'. It was an unusually warm and very quiet evening. It seemed as if a summer breeze had decided to visit the island in the middle of winter.

I went to sleep but was woken up by a massive earthquake. I rushed to my parents asking if they had felt anything, but they had not. But then the sirens from the fire engines could be heard, confirming my suspicion that something extraordinary was going on. A few minutes later I saw my parents standing on the balcony on the first floor of our house and I heard my father say: 'This must be Katla.'

The theory about Mount Katla is that it erupts every fifty years. The fearsome volcano had lain dormant since 1918. However, Mount Katla is the biggest volcano on the Icelandic mainland. This outburst was much closer, only about a kilometre away from us. We phoned the police and were informed that a volcanic eruption had started on the island. Because of the stormy weather on the previous day, the entire fleet was in the harbour. We learned from the police headquarters that families were expected to gather and go to the harbour immediately.

A swift evacuation was called for, and that night more than 5,000 people, including my mother, my youngest sister and me, sailed for the mainland towards the break of dawn. The evacuation proceeded calmly and efficiently. I have been told by my youngest sister that I was wearing a dark blue velvet jacket and carrying a chess set in a plastic bag. There was also a book, *My 60 Memorable Games*.

As our ship was about to leave, I saw a teacher of mine, a man in his early twenties, who was considered to be quite a ladies' man, an important status when you are 15 or 16 years old. He was puffing on a cigarette and gazing at the row of lava fountains that were so close to one another that they looked like an unbroken wall of fire. He looked at me and delivered a one-liner I've been unable to forget: 'This is definitely a stamp.' His prophecy was spot-on, as the Icelandic post would indeed commemorate the historic outburst with a stamp.

Slowly we sailed away past the brand new fissures that were expanding every minute, spewing hot lava at a temperature of 1,000° C. The fine ash was pouring down on the people who were standing on the deck of the ship. I did not sleep at all that night, but kept staring at Heimaey. From afar the island seemed like a gigantic fireball. In about five hours we reached Thorlakshöfn, where there was a lot of turmoil and chaos, with buses from the Red Cross all over the place. We were picked up by my cousin's husband, Einar Kvaran. Reykjavik was only 60 kilometres away. There was a lot to talk about. Whilst waiting for our ship, Einar had been watching the convoy of ships coming in and then sailing away. 'It all seemed as if it was by some divine order', he said.

It was good to be back in Reykjavik. I sat in his house for a long time listening to the conversation, which was sometimes halted by fresh news of the eruption from the radio. Finally I sneaked out, took the bus to the city centre and met a few friends. At five o'clock in the evening we went to the Tonabio cinema to see *Midnight Cowboy*. The lights went out and I somehow welcomed the darkness. Then I fell asleep. When I woke up, a bus ride had taken Dustin Hoffman and Jon Voight to Florida.

Chapter Four

Njal called out to Skarphedinn -
'Whither art thou going, kinsman?'
'On a sheep hunt', he said.
'So it was once before,' said Njal, 'but then ye hunted men.'
Njal's Saga

There were some hopes that Bobby Fischer would participate in the Chess Olympiad in Nice in the south of France in the summer of 1974 as a member of the U.S. team. He had asked for a special building to play his games. For reasons that are easy to understand that was a request that the organizers could not comply with and in the end he didn't play. While the FIDE Congress, which was held during the Olympiad, was in progress he sent a cable proposing conditions for the upcoming World Championship match. There were 179 numbered paragraphs covering every conceivable aspect and detail. Three were of utmost importance:
1. The match should continue until one player wins 10 games, without counting draws.
2. There is no limit to the total number of games played.
3. In the case of a 9-9 score, the champion retains his title and the prize fund is split equally.

FIDE found a compromise allowing the match to continue until 10 wins, but said it would not last longer than 36 games and rejected the 9-9 clause. Fischer's defence of his title became less and less probable by the day and on June 27 he cabled FIDE President Max Euwe:

As I made clear in my telegram to the FIDE delegates, the match conditions I proposed were non-negotiable. Mr. Cramer informs me that the rules of the winner being the first player to win ten games, draws not counting, unlimited number of games and if nine wins to nine match is drawn with champion regaining title and prize fund split equally were rejected by the FIDE delegates. By so doing FIDE has decided against my participating in the 1975 world chess championship. I therefore resign my FIDE world chess champion title.
Sincerely, Bobby Fischer.

Little is known about Fischer's preparation for the title defence that never took place. In the November 1974 issue of *Chess Life and Review* a letter appeared from him to Larry Evans for his column. It does shed some light on his working regimen. It is vintage Bobby Fischer:

Dear Larry,

I have a question or two for you. In June/74, p. 398, you state in answer to Larry Jadczak, 'It certainly does (draw). A very neat resource too.'

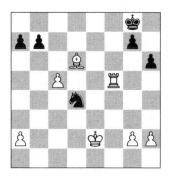

This is typical of your disappointing tendency to give superficial incorrect answers. After 29.♔d3 ♘xf5 30.♗e5! Black has a very long way to go before a draw. As a matter of fact, to me, Black's game looks hopeless: i.e., 30...♔f7 31.♔e4 ♘e7 (or 31...g6 32.♗f4 h5 33.♔e5 etc. wins) 32.♗c3! followed by ♔e5 wins. Maybe you'll still try and demonstrate some rinky-dink draw to your readers in this endgame, but remember you're not fooling me one bit – Black is dead lost.

I'm also enclosing a copy of Mr. Cramer's compilation of the Rules of the World Championship matches, and a copy of my telegram to the FIDE delegates for your information and enlightenment.

In April/74, p. 271, you state my rules are not fair. What nonsense! As if I had some great advantage because of the nine to nine tie clause. Alex Binder wrote, 'In Jan/74, p.30, a cablegram from Bobby Fischer to FIDE stated: "Urge adoption of ten wins to decide 1975 match, draws not counting, champion to retain title in nine wins to nine." This means that the champion needs only nine wins and the challenger must win by at least two. Do you feel this fair and why?' Your answer: 'No, it isn't fair. The whole idea of not counting draws is to eliminate a draw match. Historically the first player to win six games was good enough for Lasker, Capablanca, and Alekhine. Why isn't it good enough for Bobby Fischer?'

Okay. Here's my answer to Mr. Binder and then to you, Larry. Mr. Binder should have read more carefully, because he seems under the illusion that if 9 wins to 9, I win the match. That's a big difference. If my match with Spassky would have been 12-12, he would have retained the title – not won the match (and not even having to win a single game at that, if it turned out every game was a draw). The money would be split equally and the match declared a draw – but Spassky would have kept the title. Okay? Nothing unfair there! Then Mr. Binder says, 'the challenger must win by at least two'. When the champion gets 9 points, the match isn't automatically over, although at that stage his title is secure. It continues until he wins 10 games, unless the challenger wins 9 first to tie him. This is much the same as the first Petrosian-Spassky match, when Petrosian got the needed 12 points before 24 games were played: his title was secure, but the match continued until he got at least 12½ or Spassky tied him 12 to 12.

Now to your answer: 'No, it isn't fair. The whole idea of not counting draws is to eliminate a draw match.' Nonsense! The whole idea is to make sure the players draw blood by winning games, and the spectators get their money's worth. And most importantly as an accurate test of who is the world's best player.

Then you say: 'Historically the first player to win six games was good enough for Lasker, Capablanca and Alekhine. Why isn't it good enough for Bobby Fischer?'

What was good enough for them is not necessarily always good enough for me and I'm sure if they were alive today the feeling would be mutual. The real question is: which is the best title system?

But if you go back why isn't what was good enough for Steinitz, Tchigorin, Lasker (too), Gunsberg, Zukertort, etc., good enough for Larry Evans? Because they all played under the ten win system I proposed (and some matches with the 9-9 tie clause). Incidentally, Larry, the Capa-Alekhine match did have a draw clause at 5-5. Yes, Alekhine had to win by 6-4 to take the title just the same as my match proposal. So you don't know what you're talking about altogether on the subject.

The Russians are also making a big to-do about this tie clause, even though they are well aware from their own books of these facts. Yet they pretend that I'm asking for an unprecedented advantage! (See page 18 Ten Champions of the World, Moscow 1972, in Russian for Capa-Alekhine regulations – photocopy enclosed.)

In conclusion I would like to answer on a last wild rumour that the

Russians are busily spreading – namely that in 1971 when FIDE changed the match system to the first player to win six games (no tie clause, effective 1975) that this was my proposal and at my behest. This is completely untrue. I also proposed ten wins at that time and, as a matter of fact, I proposed that the ten win system go into effect for the 1972 title match! I am responsible for what I told Mr. Edmondson (the U.S. representative to FIDE) not for the compromise he and FIDE worked out without my approval or even knowledge. These are the facts – if anyone is interested in those.

In the January issue of 1975 another Bobby Fischer letter to Evans appeared in the pages of *Chess Life and Review*:

I have another question. I'm sure I'm wrong, but in Karpov-Pritchett, Nice Olympiad 1974, this position was reached:

Pritchett played 22...exf4? and eventually lost. Doesn't 22...♞e2+ bust White? For example 23.♖xe2 ♝xe2 24.♛xe2 ♛xc4 and if 25.♝f1? ♛d4+. Or if 24.♞xe5 ♖d1+ (or 24...♝d3! – less effective is 24...♝xc4 25.♝e3 – 25.♞xd3 ♖xd3 and Black's initiative is decisive. Better in this line is 25.♝e3 ♝xe4, though hopeless for White in the long run) 25.♚f2 ♝xc4 26.♛c2 (best) 26...♛b6+! 27.♝e3 (or 27.♚f3? ♖xe5 28.♝e3 ♖xa1! etc.) 27...♖xa1! 28.♝xb6 ♖a2 29.♛xa2 ♝xa2 with a won endgame for Black.

By the time this is published my analysis may have appeared under a different name, because I've shown it to a few people. Please show me what I've overlooked.
Regards,
Bobby
A: Thanks again for writing. Good to know you're alive and well.

I recall having read somewhere that Bobby saw more or less the same variations given in the magazine *Deutsche Schachzeitung*, which quoted Robert Byrne from a column he wrote in *The New York Times*.

In the autumn of 1974 Anatoly Karpov became Bobby Fischer's official challenger by beating Viktor Kortchnoi 12½-11½ in the Candidates' Final match in Moscow with three wins, two losses and 19 draws. The next news was that the Chess Federation of the Philippines, backed by President Marcos, offered the sum of $5 million in prize-money to hold the World Championship match between Fischer and Karpov in Manila, an amount almost unheard of in sports events.

In the meantime the U.S. Chess Federation was still fighting for Bobby's conditions. At a special FIDE Congress, held in March 1975 in the Netherlands, it was accepted that the match should be of unlimited duration, but the 9-9 clause was once again rejected by a narrow margin of 35 votes to 32. In the end Bobby Fischer was stripped of his title and in the spring of 1975 Anatoly Karpov was crowned the 12th World Champion. This was a tragedy for chess and for Bobby Fischer.

A new era of Soviet dominance in chess began, but most of the 'old guard', such as Spassky, Petrosian and Tal, took a back seat now. The exception was Viktor Kortchnoi, who seemed reborn following his defection to the West in July 1976.

The young Anatoly Karpov was playing great chess in the years 1971-74. In 1974 he was clearly the best player within the Soviet Union and his match with Fischer had promised to be exceptionally fascinating. His 7-4 Candidates' match victory over Spassky was just as impressive as Fischer's win against Spassky two years earlier. Spassky later commented that this was the best match Karpov ever played. As an interesting aside it may be mentioned that Efim Geller, Spassky's helping hand in the Reykjavik match, was all of a sudden appointed as Karpov's second before and during the match.

The prospect Bobby Fischer was facing in a match with Karpov was totally different from what he had faced on the road to the crown. He would no longer have the advantage of youth and he had not played a single official game during his reign as World Champion. In the end the burden of going back into the fray and facing a new opponent proved too heavy for him. Inevitably, in the years that followed, the question kept being asked: What would have happened if he had played? Why did he not just let go and play?

Garry Kasparov has stated that Bobby was afraid of Karpov and that the latter would have had good chances of winning. That seems to be a self-serving opinion. To my mind, Bobby was mainly afraid of himself. Over the years he had developed what Mikhail Botvinnik called 'a morbid fear of the chessboard'. He was afraid to lose control by making concessions. The conditions he had proposed for the match were not terribly unfair, but the Soviets had learned their lesson from Reykjavik and were determined not to give in to any of Bobby's 'whims'. There is one detail of importance that Karpov explained later concerning the length of the match: Bobby always had the idea that after three months of play without a decision the players would be allowed to rest. This would have made such a seemingly endless match even more complicated for any prospective organizer.

Bobby badly needed a guiding hand like he had in the person of Ed Edmondson during the Palma Interzonal in 1970 and the Candidates' matches in 1971, but there was no one around to take on that role. Did the U.S. Chess Federation fail in their support of Fischer? It seems to me that they were fighting for their man all the time. As for the outcome of the match that never was, I am totally convinced that Fischer would have won against Karpov in 1975. He might have been out of practice and a bit rusty, not having played an official game since the 1972 match, but in the long run he would have proved to be the stronger player.

In 1975 Karpov had not yet matured into the player he later became. His dull performance in Milan later that year, 16 draws in 21 games, reveals weaknesses that Fischer would have capitalized on. Karpov endured great difficulties in many games against Viktor Kortchnoi in their 1974 Candidates' Final match.

There are other facets that deserve attention. In the ten years that he was World Champion from 1975 to 1985, Karpov did not lose a single game against any of his countrymen whilst playing abroad. Speculating about the openings that might have been played, we may guess that Karpov had most probably prepared the Breyer Variation of the Ruy Lopez as his main weapon against Bobby's king's pawn, but there Fischer had leanings towards playing the Exchange Variation and might have taken him into different territory.

On the other hand, Karpov had made a habit of brilliantly defeating Najdorf players with the modest 6.♗e2 system. He was much better prepared in his openings than Bobby's earlier opponents, and no doubt there would have been many problems to be solved. Bobby would have been forced to make changes in his play and repertoire, just like he did when facing Spassky. His influences in the 1972 match were varied and included Robert

Hübner, Semyon Furman, Alla Kushnir, and the Alekhine-Capablanca match in 1927. In the 21st match game he even picked up an idea from a game Adolf Anderssen played in the romantic era of chess in the late 19th century.

In 1975 Karpov had already brought something new to the game of chess with his unique and highly efficient prophylactic measures both in the middlegame and in technical positions. Still, to my mind, Bobby's powerful concentration, his capacity for hard work, his playing skill and his pure energy would have given him the better chances.

But the match never took place. What a loss. And Bobby Fischer slid into obscurity.

Chapter Five

*'It joys me, brother-in-law,' says Skarphedinn, 'to think that if thou gettest
away thou wilt avenge me.'*
Njal's Saga

I don't know when exactly I gave up hope for Fischer's return to the chessboard, but there is no doubt about the immediate and unmistakable
effect that the 1972 match had on the strongest Icelandic players. The country's only grandmaster, Fridrik Olafsson, decided to turn professional again
at the end of 1973. Another notable player, Gudmundur Sigurjonsson, then
considered to be in the same category as Ulf Andersson and Jan Timman,
started his quest for the grandmaster title in the autumn of 1973, having finished law school. He fulfilled his ambition at Hastings in January
1975 ahead of English players like Tony Miles and William Hartston, who
were competing for the £5,000 Slater award for becoming the first British
grandmaster.

Both Fridrik and Gudmundur were perfect role models and inspirational
for the younger Icelandic players. Gudmundur would sometimes pay a visit
to the Reykjavik chess club and explain his most recent games to us. He
would refer to the Soviet weekly magazine 64 and consequently we became
subscribers. At this time I was already making a habit of winning nearly all
the chess tournaments I took part in in Iceland, but following in my foot-
steps was a younger player by the name of Margeir Petursson. Later Jon
Arnason joined us and then finally Johann Hjartarson.

This young and ambitious group became a formidable force in the
eighties and early nineties. It was always fun to travel with these guys. At
the Chess Olympiad in 1986 in Dubai we finished fifth, an excellent result
that was immortalized in a nicely-produced book full of pictures and games.
Next we were eighth in 1990 in Novi Sad and fifth to seventh in 1992 in
Manila. Johann surpassed all expectations by sharing first place with Valery
Salov at the Interzonal in Szirak in 1987 and then defeating Viktor Kortchnoi in the first leg of the Candidates' matches in 1988 in Saint John. This
feat was so spectacular that a performance at the National Theatre was inter-
rupted to tell the spectators the good news from Canada.

Having become World Champion without playing a title match in 1975,
Anatoly Karpov was a very active champion who achieved excellent results.

His style was a bit dry and he was seen as a typical representative of the Soviet Union under Brezhnev's rule. It seems to me that when Viktor Kortchnoi defected to the West in 1976, he took over Fischer's role of the lone fighter against the Soviet system in the public's mind. Kortchnoi was also fully aware of the importance of theatricals, as his two highly-publicized matches with Karpov in 1978 and 1981 revealed. In this stage of his career Kortchnoi had absolutely fantastic results. With unerring determination he won his Candidates' matches against Petrosian, Polugaevsky and Spassky to qualify for the World Championship match, his bitter fight with Karpov in Baguio City in 1978.

In 1979 Garry Kasparov appeared on the scene. The 16-year-old boy from Baku won the Banja Luka tournament in Yugoslavia, demonstrating really powerful chess. From then on he became a dominant force in chess. I consider his five matches with Karpov in the period 1984-1991 to be the highlight of creative chess in the last century.

Shortly after the Chess Olympiad in Manila in 1992, where Kasparov in effect put on a chess exhibition and 16-year-old Russian debutant Vladimir Kramnik scored 8½ out of 9, dropping a draw only to the author, the news broke that a Bobby Fischer comeback was imminent.

Fischer's comeback twenty years after the match in Reykjavik came too late. The press conference in Sveti Stefan, where he first appeared in public again, was a bad omen. Sporting a beard and having gained weight Fischer belligerently addressed the questions of journalists and caused a worldwide stir when he defiantly spat on a document faxed to him by the U.S. Treasury Department. The letter called on him not to play a chess match in Yugoslavia and to respect the embargo against the war-torn country and refrain from any economic activities. It was obvious right away that he would have to pay a heavy price for his erratic behaviour.

Still, out of the 30 games he played with Spassky in Sveti Stefan and Belgrade, Bobby Fischer won 10, losing five and drawing 15. Most of his wins had his trademark simple and elegant style, but some of his errors, especially in the first stage of the match, would not have been found in his games earlier in his career.

The prize fund for the match in Sveti Stefan and Belgrade, provided by Serbian banker Jezdemir Vasilievic, was $5 million. Vasilievic, a man with a dubious reputation, who later had to flee the country, had called the match an open war against the United Nations embargo. Fischer's winner's share was $3.35 million. Most of that amount was put into his UBS bank account in Zurich, Switzerland.

Kasparov, the then World Champion, was not impressed by the quality of the games. He talked about 'chess from the seventies', and speaking about Fischer he said, 'He is an alien.' It is tempting to mention that Spassky was always a great match player and that Kasparov's results against him, even if he was still young at the time, were not too impressive. Out of his seven games with Spassky he won twice, lost twice and they made three draws. Kasparov played with the white pieces in four of those games.

Bobby Fischer's most valuable contribution to the second match against Spassky and the lasting inheritance of his comeback may have been his new digital chess clock. Adding time whenever a move was made, the clock was a great invention that had a revolutionary impact on modern tournament chess.

There was another invention of his that he was obsessed by. After the second match against Spassky, he was expected to play some more matches, but he was no longer interested in classical chess. When he engaged in discussions with the Polgar family to play a match against one of the three famous sisters, he demanded that they would play a 'Fischer-Random' match, a type of chess also called Chess960, in which the pieces start in random positions on the back rank. In June 1996 Fischer went to Buenos Aires to promote the game. There it was announced that he would play a match with his friend Eugenio Torre. However, here too, he had a fight with the organizers and his plans fell through.

Towards the end of 1999 I attended a party thrown by Mal og mynd (Language and Image), a small Reykjavik publishing company. Together with Bragi Halldorsson and Jon Torfason, I had co-written a book about an Icelandic chess legend, Benony Benediktsson. He was a truly original player who had made a name for himself in Iceland by drawing with the Soviet champion at the time, Mark Taimanov, and other strong players like Georgy Ilivitsky, Milan Matulovic and Yuri Balashov.

Benony had a very original chess style and some of his witticisms, mimicked in his slightly odd voice, can still be heard in Icelandic chess circles. Both Bragi Halldorsson and Jon Torfason are strong players, also well known in Iceland for their efforts to publish the Icelandic sagas. Our conversation that evening turned to the interviews that Bobby Fischer had given to Hungarian and Filipino radio stations, aggressive soliloquies that spread like wildfire on the Internet.

My home was nearby and I invited them over to listen. Fischer was furious that his belongings that were stored at the Bekins storage house in Pasadena had been confiscated, but his rage was not only directed against the owner of the company. His anti-Semitic rants were particularly unsettling. Bragi and Jon were both shocked by Bobby's anger-stricken voice. This was a very desperate man. It seemed to us he must be mentally ill. We decided to contact Gudmundur Thorarinsson, the organizer of the 1972 match, and the following evening we paid him a visit with printouts from the interviews. There we decided that a meeting with the U.S. ambassador in Iceland was called for and I was asked to draft a letter:

Reykjavik, the 15th of November 1999
To Ambassador Barbara J. Griffiths
By writing this letter we the undersigned ask you to look into the matter of your countryman Bobby Fischer, world chess champion 1972-1975.

   In September 1972 Bobby Fischer was crowned world chess champion, having beaten Boris Spassky in Reykjavik 12½-8½, thus breaking the Soviet hegemony that had lasted from the year 1948 and brought the chess world no fewer than five Soviet world champions. On his return to the U.S. Bobby Fischer together with the swimmer Mark Spitz was hailed a national hero. To the greatest disappointment of his admirers Fischer went into a kind of a self-imposed exile after the match and did not play a single public game for 20 years.

   In 1992 he travelled to Sveti Stefan, a summer resort in Yugoslavia, to play a rematch with Boris Spassky. In the words of columnist Charles Krauthammer writing for *Time* magazine, this was the greatest comeback since Napoleon Bonaparte sailed a single-masted flat-bottom from the island of Elba in the year 1815.

Before the match U.S. authorities responded by sending him the following telegram:

Department of the Treasury
Washington
Aug 21, 1992

Order to Provide Information and Cease and Desist Activities
FAC No. 129405
Dear Mr. Fischer:
It has come to our attention that you are planning to play a chess match for

a cash prize in the Federal Republic of Yugoslavia (Serbia and Montenegro) (hereinafter 'Yugoslavia') against Boris Spassky on or about September 1, 1992. As a U.S. citizen, you are subject to the prohibitions under Executive Order 12810, dated June 5, 1992, imposing sanctions against Serbia and Montenegro. The United States Department of the Treasury, Office of Foreign Assets Control ('FAC'), is charged with enforcement of the Executive Order.

The Executive Order prohibits U.S. persons from performing any contract in support of a commercial project in Yugoslavia, as well as from exporting services to Yugoslavia. The purpose of this letter is to inform you that the performance of your agreement with a corporate sponsor in Yugoslavia to play chess is deemed to be in support of that sponsor's commercial activity. Any transactions engaged in for this purpose are outside the scope of General License No. 6, which authorizes only transactions to travel, not to business or commercial activities. In addition, we consider your presence in Yugoslavia for this purpose to be an exportation of services to Yugoslavia in the sense that the Yugoslav sponsor is benefiting from the use of your name and reputation.

Violations of the Executive Order are punishable by civil penalties not to exceed $10,000 per violation, and by criminal penalties not to exceed $250,000 per individual, 10 years in prison, or both. You are hereby directed to refrain from engaging in any of the activities described above. You are further requested to file a report with this office within 10 business days of your receipt of this letter, outlining the facts and circumstances surrounding any and all transactions relating to your scheduled chess match in Yugoslavia against Boris Spassky. The report should be addressed to: The U.S. Department of the Treasury, Office of Foreign Assets Control, Enforcement Division, 1500 Pennsylvania Avenue, N.W., Annex – 2nd floor, Washington D.C. 20220. If you have any questions regarding this matter, please contact Merete M. Evans at (202) 622-2430.

Sincerely,

(signed)

R. Richard Newcomb

Director

Office of Foreign Assets Control

On the 15th of December the same year a federal warrant for Bobby Fischer's arrest was issued:

Federal Warrant for the Arrest of Bobby Fischer

Warrant for Arrest Dickey J.
United States District Court
for the District of Columbia

UNITED STATES of AMERICA
vs.
ROBERT JAMES FISCHER

Criminal No. CR 92-475-01 GJC
Name and Address of Person to be Arrested:
ROBERT JAMES FISCHER
No Known Address
NO PDID
DOB: 3/9/43
To U.S. Marshall or any authorized agent:
YOU ARE HEREBY COMMANDED to arrest the above named person and bring that person before the nearest available magistrate to answer the charge(s) listed below:
Description of Charge:
50 USC §§1701, 1702, and 1705 INTERNATIONAL EMERGENCY ECONOMIC POWERS ACT
[stamp] received [date illegible] '93 U.S. Marshall
Ordered by Patrick U. Atteridge
United States Magistrate Judge
date 12/15/92

It is very clear that the case that we have been looking into has inflicted upon Bobby Fischer a great personal tragedy. He was unable to attend the funeral of his mother in 1997 and his sister who died last year. A storage room he rented in Pasadena was recently broken up and all his belongings confiscated and auctioned for a meagre debt of somewhere around $400. Fischer had apparently done everything possible to pay this debt, but with his closest relatives gone he was unable to do so. His memorabilia consisted among other things of valuable prizes he had been given during his career, personal letters from heads of state such as president Richard Nixon and Ferdinand Marcos etc.

To the best of our knowledge Fischer is living in Budapest in Hungary. By bringing this matter to your attention we the undersigned are attempting to have the case against this individual dropped. For seven years he has been an international fugitive from justice. Obviously a troubled genius but nevertheless a true and honest sportsman who in the summer of 1972 did his country a great service by beating a Soviet world champion in a high-profile match. He seems to be the only person involved in that match in Sveti Stefan/Belgrade 1992 to have been indicted.

Signed: Gudmundur G. Thorarinsson, Askell Örn Karason, Helgi Olafsson.

We received an answer from the U.S. embassy in Reykjavik in mid-December 1999 and were invited to discuss the matter with the ambassador at the embassy in early 2000. It was decided that I would go there together with Gudmundur Thorarinsson and the president of the Icelandic Chess Federation, Askell Örn Karason, whose presence as spokesman for the Icelandic chess community we deemed necessary. As I explained to the ambassador at the meeting, we decided to inform the media beforehand.

On a frosty morning in early January we stood for a while outside the embassy with a few cameramen and some other members of the press. The meeting lasted for more than two hours, but Askell had to leave early and Gudmundur and I did most of the talking.

Both here and later I was impressed by the way Gudmundur managed to sway his audience. As well as the ambassador Barbara Griffiths, two officers from the embassy took part in the meeting, taking notes. Gudmundur is a huge fan of Shakespeare and at times he would refer to his favourite poet in describing Bobby: 'I could be bounded in a nutshell, and count myself a king of infinite space' was one of his favourite quotations from *Hamlet*.

A few weeks later we were notified by the embassy that the warrant for Bobby's arrest would never expire. I had a talk with then-PM David Oddsson during a rapid chess tournament in which Kasparov and Anand participated. Oddsson told me and Jan Timman, who was standing next to me, that Fischer's case had been brought up at a very high level. He did not tell us where or when, but I recall that both he and U.S. President Bill Clinton attended a NATO meeting in Madrid in 1997. At that time the answer given through an official was that this was not the right time to do anything.

When Bill Clinton's term was coming to an end, as is a recognized practice, he pardoned a few U.S. citizens, some with rather shady business dealings on their record. Bobby was not pardoned. No one in the U.S. would take up his cause. Oddsson promised us that he would let his staff work on the matter.

Our good intentions abruptly came to a halt shortly after September 11, 2001, when a brand-new interview with Bobby Fischer surfaced on the Internet, in which he glorified the attacks on the Twin Towers. The most quoted words from his anti-American and anti-Semitic rant were 'This is all wonderful news. It is time to finish off the U.S. once and for all.' There were some doubts about the authenticity of the voice, but I immediately knew this was Bobby Fischer.

Chapter Six

*'Ours is no woman's nature,' says Skarphedinn, 'that we should fly into a rage
at every little thing.'*
Njal's Saga

On July 13, 2004, Bobby Fischer was about to board flight JL 745 from
Narita airport in Tokyo to Manila in the Philippines. He had been criss-
crossing between the two countries as his residence permit would expire
every three months. After the match in Sveti Stefan and Belgrade in 1992
Bobby had been living under the radar in Budapest. It is known that he was
a guest of the Polgar family a few times, and occasionally he met with Lajos
Portisch, but his closest companion there was probably a relatively weak
Hungarian chess player, a businessman by the name of Janos Rigo.

The family of Hungarian-born physicist Paul Nemenyi, thought to be
Bobby's biological father, was also living in Budapest, but there is no evidence of any communication. During and after the match with Spassky in
1992 Bobby was said to be in love with Zita Raiczanyi, a Hungarian chess
player who had written him a letter pleading with him to play again. There
was no doubt that she was instrumental in getting him back to chess. They
had a prolonged affair, but not for the first time in his life Bobby's manners
failed him and much to his chagrin Zita broke off the relationship.

In 2004 he was leading a double life. In Tokyo he lived with Miyoko
Watai, the General Secretary of the Japanese Chess Association whom he had
met for the first time in the Japanese capital in 1973. And he regularly stayed
in the Philippines. According to some sources he had fathered a daughter
there, named Jinky, with a girlfriend called Marilyn Young in 2001. Bobby's
friend, the first Asian grandmaster Eugenio Torre, was living in Manila and
he probably played a key role in getting Bobby to do some of his infamous
interviews that started in 1999.

At Narita airport on this day in July Bobby Fischer's life took a dramatic
turn when his passport, issued at the U.S. embassy in Zürich in 1997, was
being scanned. After 9/11 all the major institutions in the States were mobi-
lized to catch enemies of the state and the former chess hero fallen from
grace was one of them. It was almost inevitable that in the end they would
get him. The guard at the gate inspecting Bobby's passport called for assistance. Bobby was thrown into custody and the news made worldwide head-

lines: Bobby Fischer was being held at Narita airport. The first photograph of Fischer in many years appeared in the international press, the picture of an angry-looking man resembling a wolf.

His account of the incident was published on the now-defunct Bobby Fischer website. There was no indication of who authored the account, but because of the tone and the abundance of details no one doubted that these were the words of Bobby Fischer himself: 'On July 13th 2004 at about 5.25 pm. Robert James Fischer ('Bobby' Fischer) entered the Japanese immigration dept. on his way to Japan Airlines flight JL 745 departing from Tokyo/Narita airport at 6.20 pm for Manila, Philippines. Bobby gave the immigration lady his passport and she quickly stamped his exit visa. However, he'd forgotten to fill out the immigration departure form. She told him to fill it out at a nearby writing stand. He took it over there and filled it out. But when Bobby returned a couple of minutes later an immigration man had replaced her. Bobby gave him back his passport and the filled out immigration form. However, when the immigration man put his passport under a special light a beep went off or was set off and Bobby was detained.

Bobby was asked to take a nearby seat while they found out what was the problem. Bobby took the seat and as he was waiting he heard someone on the phone fiercely barking instructions to an immigration official. The immigration official kept repeating in a loud militaristic manner, 'hai, hai!' After Bobby had waited there about 15 minutes or so he told the immigration official talking on the phone that his plane was leaving shortly and that he didn't want to miss the flight.

By now all pretense of civility was gone and the immigration official fairly shouted at Bobby, 'I know that, sit down!' and went back to his bullshit phone call. After waiting there on his seat for about half an hour or so altogether Bobby was told to accompany various immigration security officials. Bobby went with them through the office to the left of the immigration exit counters and then down a ways to an elevator. Bobby and the security officials took the elevator down at least one floor. Then Bobby and the immigration security officials took a long walk down the dark and narrow corridor to Bobby was told not where.

The atmosphere had turned threatening, foreboding, hostile and sinister. The place was completely apart and isolated from other passengers. There were only immigration types. Bobby asked, 'Where are we going?' He was told they were going to an office to talk. Bobby stopped walking and said, 'What's the problem?' Bobby was told that he should just go to the office to talk. Bobby said, 'About what?' Bobby was told, 'We just talk.'

At some stage a young, extremely fat, half-Japanese and half-Latino translator made his portly appearance. By now Bobby said, 'I'm not moving until I know what this is all about.' Bobby tried to start walking in the direction of where he'd come from. He was blocked by a smirking young immigration security type. Bobby was now surrounded by about at least 4 or 5 immigration security types plus the translator. The security types kept coming and going, but overall their number slowly increased...

Bobby demanded to know if he was under arrest and if so what were the charges against him. Bobby said he wasn't moving until he found out what this was all about. Over and over and over again Bobby was asked if he wished to see someone from the U.S. embassy. Bobby was told he had a right to contact the U.S. embassy. Bobby was told maybe they can help you. Bobby always answered immediately and vehemently and with finality that he did not wish to see anyone from the U.S. embassy nor did he wish to contact the U.S. embassy.

Bobby explained that the U.S. embassy was itself the problem, not the solution. Bobby explained that the U.S. government is evil and that they were out to 'get' him. Even the translator conceded to Bobby in Spanish that in his opinion Bush is a monster! Bobby asked to call a friend many times but they refused. After everyone was standing in the hallway for about 45 minutes or so, a half-crazed security official came out with Bobby's passport and they showed Bobby what they said was his arrest warrant. But they wouldn't let Bobby touch it.

It appeared to be a 2-page document. It was in Japanese and English. Bobby tried to read the first page from a distance, but only got a glimpse of the second page. The first page said that Bobby had illegally entered Japan and illegally left Japan!!! Bobby asked, 'When did I illegally enter Japan?' He was told it was all there on the arrest warrant. Bobby said, 'Where's the date I illegally entered?' Bobby said maybe it's in Japanese but that he didn't see it in English. They said it's there in English too.

They said that everything on the arrest warrant was in Japanese and English. If the date when Bobby allegedly illegally entered Japan was in English or Western numerals Bobby sure didn't see it. The older, half-crazed, higher-level immigration official told Bobby that his passport was not valid. Bobby said, 'Since when is it not valid? You mean it was not valid when I entered Japan a few months ago?' The kook answered, 'That's right!' Bobby continued, 'It wasn't valid when I entered Japan 3 months ago? Since when hasn't it been valid?' The kook answered, 'Oh, long before that!'

Bobby pressed on. 'Since when hasn't it been valid?' The kook answered since last November!!! The immigration kook said that the U.S. government told them that Bobby's passport wasn't valid since then. (Let's leave aside for another occasion the extremely important constitutional question of whether the U.S. government purely by edict has the right to restrict, revoke or invalidate etc. a U.S. passport that is otherwise perfectly valid, i.e. is not counterfeit or forged, has not been altered, has not expired, is not being used by a person other than to whom it was originally issued to, etc. It's not hard to imagine where Bobby would stand on that issue.)

The kooky higher-level immigration official then took out his immigration stamp and stamped Bobby's entry visa and Bobby's exit visa in the passport invalid. All this without any investigation or getting Bobby's side of the story. Simply on the word of the great United States! Bobby found all of this to be slightly incredible because Bobby's passport was perfectly valid in every way with about 2 and a half years left on it till it expired on January 23rd of 2007.

Furthermore, in October and November of 2003 Bobby had personally visited the Bern, Switzerland U.S. embassy (the same U.S. embassy that had originally issued the 10-year passport No. Z7792702 to Bobby on January 24, 1997) because Bobby's passport was almost completely full with almost no place left for more visa stamps. Bobby had been sternly advised on several occasions by both Japanese and Hong Kong immigration officials that his passport urgently needed to get more pages put into it immediately so there would be space for more visa stamps.

In about late October of 2003 Bobby told the people in the U.S. embassy at Bern, Switzerland that he needed more pages for his passport, otherwise he soon wouldn't be able to travel for lack of space to make visa stamps. After about ten days and many phone calls back and forth and at least two visits to the embassy in Bern they finally gave Bobby the extra pages for his passport. The U.S. embassy at Bern never explained to Bobby what the delay was all about except to say that the State Department needed time to make the decision whether or not to give him the extra pages. To Bobby's surprise, on November 6, 2003 they gave him the 24 or so extra page insert which they professionally bound into his passport free of charge! Such service! But that was about 8 months ago in neutral Switzerland. Now Bobby was in U.S.-occupied – excuse us – U.S.-controlled Japan.

Obviously the filthy Jew-controlled U.S. government preferred to illegally and criminally grab and destroy Bobby's passport only when Bobby was not in neutral Switzerland. So instead they planned to do the job elsewhere at a time and manner of their own choosing... The U.S. not only wanted to grab and destroy Bobby's U.S. passport, but far more importantly they wanted to grab and destroy Bobby too. And neutral Switzerland was not the right place to do it...

Of course, after Bobby had received his about 24-page passport insert from the U.S. embassy at Bern, Switzerland on November 6, 2003, Bobby had assumed that he was 'home free' at least until January 23, 2007, when his passport would expire. Little did Bobby suspect the devilish criminal plot that the 'moderate' Colin Powell had in store for him...

By now Bobby felt certain that there was a real possibility of his being chained and handcuffed and flown back to the filthy Jew-controlled U.S.A. with a bag over his head that very night. So he decided not to go down without a fight! The immigration officials security types and the translator told Bobby that he was being detained and/or arrested and that he had to go with them. Bobby said, 'No, I'm not moving.'

At this point Bobby was surrounded by a total of about 15 people, including the translator and a young man with a video camera out and filming. At this point the immigration security guards made their move and attacked Bobby. Bobby didn't touch them until they attacked him first. Of course, Bobby was overwhelmed. A short scuffle broke out where Bobby tried to bite one of the guards but only bit into his heavy shirt (but anyway, Bobby could tell by the expression on the guard's face that he felt it).

Bobby also got in a few good kicks before they subdued him. They then put a black or brown bag over Bobby's head and lifted him up by his legs and arms and carried him in a horizontal position to wherever they were taking him. Hands and arms and legs were all over Bobby, pummeling him, pushing him, twisting him, suffocating him. One or more guards was deliberately inflicting great pain by constantly twisting Bobby's right arm. Bobby was sure it was going to break, but it didn't. Also Bobby felt one or more guards were trying to put handcuffs on him.

Finally Bobby was dumped into a room where one or more guards was sitting on or otherwise putting strong pressure on Bobby's back. All of the air was forced out of Bobby's lungs. What very little breathing Bobby could even attempt to do was also blocked by the black or brown bag on his head. Bobby shouted over and over again that 'I can't breathe, I can't breathe', but they paid no attention. Bobby twisted his head back and forth furiously, all the while shouting, 'I can't breathe, I can't breathe!' This went on for what seemed like about a minute or two. Bobby only had about a second or two left before he would have passed out and/or died. Bobby was already thinking: 'So this is how I will die. Will my friends and loved ones ever really know the truth about how I was murdered?'

What will the press say about it? It was all planned this way by the Jews... It really is true all the horror stories, all the 'suicides', all the murders in custody... It's so damned easy... it's so quick... Suddenly after what seemed like an eternity the guy or guys got off of Bobby's back and he could breathe! Apparently they'd just been taking their sweet time about robbing Bobby's belongings, taking his belt and shoes off, taking his handcuffs off, etc. Maybe they didn't want Bobby to see the handcuffs. Or maybe one or more of them wanted to kill Bobby but one or more of them didn't. Whatever, Bobby is still alive!

The bag was gone from Bobby's head, the cuffs were off and Bobby was alone in a prison cell. Bobby's belt was gone and so was his money, his wallet, shoes, etc. The young man continued to video Bobby from outside the bars for some time even after the guards left the prison cell. Now Bobby had time to survey the damage. His right arm hurt very much but apparently was not broken. His right wrist was bloodied and bruised with a good sized gash on the outside part of his right wrist about half an inch above the wrist-bone. A number of his teeth had been chipped or broken or worse in the melee. After the fight Bobby took out a piece of one of his teeth and saved it. Bobby's left cheekbone was also sore and obviously was hurt during the fight.

The next day, on July 14th, 2004 the guards came into Bobby's cell and told him that he had a visitor from the U.S. embassy in Tokyo who wanted to see him. Bobby told them he didn't want to see anyone from the U.S. embassy. They told Bobby that he had no choice. Bobby refused to go. They told Bobby that he was going to see the visitor from the U.S. embassy whether he liked it or not!

They forcefully grabbed Bobby's arms and legs and started to lift and carry him in a similar manner to the night before. Bobby was still hurting badly from the night before, so on the spot he decided to 'surrender' and go and see his unwelcome visitor without any further struggle. They took Bobby to a room (not the special 'visitors' room' where the prisoner and the visitor are separated by a glass window) where the U.S. embassy man was either already there waiting or else came in a minute or so later. The embassy man did all the talking while Bobby didn't say a word. He had

In the television studio with Pall Magnusson and Jon Arnason, explaining a game during the 1988 Reykjavik World Cup.

The stamp issued by the Icelandic Post to commemorate the historic volcanic outburst on Heimaey, the only inhabited island of the Westman Islands, on January 23, 1973.

On January 23, 1993 I became the 1973 champion of the Westman Islands, when Andri Hrolfson resigned our game that had been adjourned on the eve of the volcanic eruption 20 years before.

Accompanied by his daughters in national costume,
Gudmundur Thorarinsson, President of the Icelandic Chess
Federation, welcomes World Champion Boris Spassky at
Keflavik aiport on June 21, 1972. On the left Fridrik Olafsson,
at the time Iceland's only grandmaster.

Turning around to the arbiters, Bobby Fischer complains about
the noise in the playing hall. Boris Spassky no longer seems to
be surprised by the American's protest.

September 1972. On his way to the airport Bobby Fischer,
accompanied by Saemi Palsson and Argentinian grandmaster
Miguel Quinteros, paid a hasty visit to the National Museum, where
he signed the leather cushion on the table the match was played on.

On his arrival on March 24, 2005, Bobby Fischer is whisked
into a car. Einar Einarsson (left) and Gudmundur Thorarinsson
(also wearing a cap) get no chance to welcome him.

At a reception in Hotel Holt on April 2, 2005 Bobby is handed the Letter of Citizenship. (L. to R.) Einar Einarsson, Saemi Palsson, Bobby Fischer, Miyoko Watai, Saemi's wife Asgerdur, Gudmundur Thorarinsson, Magnus Skulason, Ingvar Asmundsson, Gardar Sverrison and I.

Bobby reunited with the table on which he won the Match of the Century.

Talking to Bobby at the reception in Hotel Holt.

in front of him on his side of the table what appeared to be the remnants of Bobby's U.S. passport. It now had numerous large holes in it along the edges. Also something appeared to be stamped on the inside of it.

The embassy man also had a photocopy of a letter or a purported letter to Bobby from the United States embassy in Manila, Philippines dated December 11, 2003 advising Bobby that his passport was revoked. The embassy man explained to Bobby with what can only be described as a deliberate tongue in cheek or mock cat that ate the canary look on his face and obvious malicious glee that since the State Department didn't know exactly where to reach Bobby they thought that this would be the best chance to notify Bobby of the revocation of his passport because they know that Bobby visits the Philippines from time to time... (Needless to say Bobby had never seen or heard of this letter before his forced meeting with the embassy man on July 14, 2004. We'll have more to say about this letter later on.)

The embassy man further explained to Bobby that the revocation of his passport would not hinder him from receiving from the U.S. embassy in Tokyo a special one-time one-trip passport only good to return to the United States... The embassy man then added that, well, if Bobby had no further questions he'd be leaving. Then he looked at Bobby intently and maliciously and with twinkling eyes shot out: 'Well, Mr. Fischer, if you have no objection I'll be taking your passport back to the embassy with me.'

This was meant to be his coup de grace or piece de resistance. What would Bobby say? What would Bobby do? If Bobby remained silent the embassy man would say that Bobby didn't object to him taking Bobby's mutilated and destroyed passport back to the embassy with him. And then by extension the embassy man would claim or imply (with a straight face) that well, maybe Mr. Fischer didn't really mind that the U.S. had grabbed and destroyed his passport because after all he knew that we had the legal right to do so...

On the other hand, if Bobby answered and said that he does object he would break his silence and then the embassy man could say that Bobby had voluntarily met with him and that they had a voluntary conversation and that Bobby didn't say this or he didn't say that or he didn't assert his rights here or he didn't assert his rights there, etc.

Bobby answered and said, 'Give me back my passport, you son of a bitch!' At which the embassy man winced and replied that oh well yes I'll leave it here with the security people with your belongings. He broke that promise about 5 minutes later when he left the Narita airport immigration lockup with Bobby's passport! Bobby asked the embassy man if he was a Jew. The embassy man said, 'Are you?' Bobby said, 'I asked you first!'

The embassy man said that oh, no he wasn't going to play that game, that he didn't have to answer that question. Bobby asked the embassy man his name. The embassy man said his first name was 'Peter'. Bobby asked, 'Peter. What's your last name?' 'Peter' told Bobby that 'that doesn't concern you!' The arrogance and criminality of the U.S. embassy people is almost unbelievable. And at just about that point their conversation came to an end and 'Peter' left their meeting room.

Immediately after 'Peter' left the immigration lock-up dept. the immigration authorities gave Bobby on behalf of 'Peter' a photocopy of the aforementioned purported letter from the U.S. embassy in Manila to 'Bobby'. But it's just a joke, of course. This purported 2-pages letter is from the embassy of the United States of America, Manila, Philippines dated December 11, 2003 to Robert James Fischer and signed by Theodore Allegra, consul of the United States of America.

Along with the letter they gave Bobby the letter's supposed 'enclosure', something called '22 CFR Ch.1 (4-1-97 Edition) Department of State' pages 252, 253, 254, 255, 256 and (presumably) 257. The absolute first time Bobby ever saw or heard of this supposed letter to him and its supposed enclosure was July 14th 2004. Bobby never ever goes to the Philippine embassy in Manila. Bobby doesn't think he's ever been there in his life! But if he ever did go there at anytime in his life it was surely many decades ago!!! It's an absolute joke. As a matter of fact and just for the record Bobby is not in the habit of visiting or calling U.S. embassies anywhere in the world. Since Bobby left the U.S.A. in about July of 1992 (and he hasn't been back to the U.S.A. since then) the only embassy he has visited was the U.S. embassy in Bern, Switzerland.

The only other exception is a one-time visit in about 1994 or 1995 to the U.S.A. library reading room in Budapest, Hungary. Bobby made the visit with Mr. Pal Benko and at Mr. Benko's urging. However, Bobby found the atmosphere there to be so oppressive and downright scary (guards, body check, bag check, etc.) that he never went there again.

Bobby's attitude has been, especially since he was indicted by the U.S. government on trumped up political charges on December 15, 1992, that the less contact with U.S. government officials the better. The last time Bobby was in the Philippines was around last summer. Months before this December 11, 2003 alleged letter was written. Bobby hasn't been back to the Philippines since then. How in the world was Bobby ever to receive or even hear about this alleged letter?...

Bobby has spent most of his time in Japan since January of 2000. He's made a few good friends and acquaintances here. He's spent hundreds of thousands of dollars visiting Japanese 'Onsen' (mineral bath). He's spent over three hundred and fifty thousand dollars working with the Seiko corporation trying to further develop his high-tech dream chess clock. He's spent a small fortune on Japanese electronic products and other Japanese products. But all this is outweighed by one lying phone call and one lying fraudulent letter from the U.S. government. Even if he lives and ever gets out of jail again he will never return to Japan again until every U.S. military base in Japan is closed and Japan is a free and independent country again.'

Bobby Fischer was kept in a cell at the airport for a few days before he was transferred to the East Japan Immigration Detention Center in Ushiku. The match in the former Yugoslavia had now come to its 'logical' conclusion. I still doubt very much that Bobby would have suffered so terribly had he not given the infamous 9/11 interview.

I called Karl Blöndal, the editor of Morgunbladid, and offered to write an article which appeared at the end of July titled: 'Bobby Fischer – an enigma.' There were petitions being signed for Bobby Fischer's release in some countries, but I had the feeling that his matter would not be solved easily. In early October I got a call from Gudmundur Thorarinsson. He had decided to invite a few friends to his house to discuss the matter. Besides me and Gudmundur, in attendance were Gudfridur Lilja Gretarsdottir, the president of the Icelandic Chess Federation, Hrafn Jökulsson, Magnus Skulason, Ingvar Asmundsson, Saemundur Palsson, Einar Einarsson, and Gardar Sverrison.

Hrafn Jökulsson was a journalist, poet and writer who from 1999 onwards organized a series of chess tournaments in Iceland and even one in Greenland. Together with a few of his friends he founded a chess club called Hrokurinn. With the support of foreign grandmasters such as Alexei Shirov and Michael Adams the club won the Icelandic league several times.

Psychiatrist Magnus Skulason was the head of Iceland's hospital for the criminally insane, and also a strong amateur chess player and collector of old chess material, books and articles. Ingvar Asmundsson, a former Icelandic chess champion, had met Bobby in Portoroz in 1958, when he was Fridrik Olafsson's second.

I had no idea why Gardar Sverrison was there. He was not known at all in chess circles, but I assumed he was drawn to the matter like so many others. I had read his book: Býr Íslendingur hér (Does an Icelander live here?) – about Leifur Möller, an Icelander who had been sent to German labour camps during World War II. If my memory does not betray me, a matter of great importance to Gardar Sverrison was a newly-released biography of Bill Clinton, in which a special mention was given to a curious detail concerning an arms deal with the Croats which the U.S. administration turned a blind eye towards in spite of a ban on all business relations with former Yugoslav states.

The U.S. Treasury Department had informed Bobby Fischer before the match in Sveti Stefan/Belgrade that by participating he would be in violation of Executive Order 12810. In effect, Bobby Fischer was the only U.S. citizen to have been indicted as the result of the U.N. sanctions against Yugoslavia, and Gudmundur was of the opinion that the best course of action was to offer Bobby a residence permit in Iceland.

This would call for the assistance of our Minister of Foreign Affairs, and in David Oddsson we quickly found a willing and eager ally. On the 15th of December, as we were having a meeting with the Japanese ambassador in Reykjavik, the news broke out that Oddson had indeed granted Bobby Fischer a residence permit. Oddsson later told Ingvar Asmundsson that within the cabinet he had not received any real support, but as it happened he was allowed to do whatever he thought necessary. In David's own words: 'From our point of view, if it is really a violation of an embargo to play chess there, then nevertheless it has no validation here because of the statute of limitation. Our view is that we find it odd to persecute a man because of a matter of this kind. The U.S. ambassador in Iceland emphasized that this was not a matter of the U.S. State Department but the U.S. Justice Department, but I said that I was not asking for permission of any kind to make this decision, however I was informing him about my decision in full respect and friendship. And I don't see any reason for people being afraid that the U.S. will ask us to hand him over because I do not believe the Americans will push it so hard as to have him handed over, in any case we would stick to the aforementioned fact – the statute of limitation – and the fact he is not breaking Icelandic law by playing chess.'

When it was suggested that Fischer received special treatment, Oddsson acknowledged this fact: 'It is quite normal that people think this individual is getting special treatment and we cannot explain it otherwise. This is a very special individual who is tied to Iceland's saga in a special way. I do not recall another case of this kind in recent years, but we also reacted differently many years ago in the case of Vladimir Ashkenazy, that was of course because he was tied to us in a special way.' Here he was referring to the fact that Ashkenazy, who decided to leave the USSR in 1963, was granted Icelandic citizenship in 1972 because he was married to an Icelandic woman.

Shortly afterwards Einar Einarsson received the following telegram:

Dear Einar,
Thank you very much for very good news. Now when the whole chess world is cowardly silent, Icelandic people made a natural and brave move to help Bobby. Congratulations. And my applause! If you need my assistance or help, please let me know. I will join with great pleasure the group of brave Icelandic people. I take the opportunity to wish you all a Merry Christmas and a Happy New Year.
Boris Spassky

We were hoping that Fischer would be freed at Christmas time. But then the world turned its attention to the Asian tsunami in the Indian Ocean that left more than 225,000 people dead in eleven countries. Some of us also had the feeling that U.S. officials in Japan were in some way intervening to delay the process. Meanwhile, Pall Magnusson had an interview with Bobby in detention in Japan on the TV station Channel 2. I helped Pall with some of the questions. One in particular took him by surprise:

Pall Magnusson: I have in front of me a recent interview with Garry Kasparov...

Fischer: [exasperated sigh]

Pall Magnusson: ...and there he takes a very positive view on 'Fischer-Random'. He says that could very well be the future of chess.

Fischer: Really?? That is a surprise because in the past he has never had anything positive to say about it. Where was this interview published?

Pall Magnusson: It was on the Internet edition of a chess magazine. I have direct quotes from the interview and Kasparov is very positive.

Fischer: That's amazing. Did he say anything about me in prison? I guess he doesn't care about that, right?

Pall Magnusson: He expresses sorrow about it and says it is a tragedy. When asked about 'Fischer-Random' he suggests that one should downsize the number of the opening positions to 20 or 30...

Fischer: Oooooh! There's the catch. [Laughs] That does not sound like he likes 'Fischer-Random' at all. It sounds like he wants to ruin 'Fischer-Random'.

Pall Magnusson: He says, 'Simply pick a position and play it for a year. Next year a different position.'

Fischer: That is exactly what I'm trying to avoid! I'm trying to put the spontaneity back. He's trying to do the same thing to 'Fischer-Random' that has happened to the old chess. I'm glad you told me that, I knew it was too good to be true.

Pall Magnusson: Let me give you another quote [reads from interview]: 'It seems to me that "Fischer-Random" is one possible way to resolve the problem. I just heard about this and also that the reaction of chess players was, strange as it may seem, negative on the whole. From my viewpoint "Fischer-Random" is entirely acceptable.' His view on this is positive.

Fischer: [Long pause] Well, I'm receiving a lot of mixed signals there. I don't like the sound... no, no, I don't trust him at all.

On the 19th of January Bobby Fischer, at the instigation of our group, wrote and signed the following letter:

Ushiku, Japan, January 19, 2005
Althingi
The Icelandic Parliament
150 Reykjavik 0 Iceland
Honorable members of Althingi:
I undersigned, Robert James Fischer, sincerely thank the Icelandic Nation for the friendship it has shown to me ever since I came to your country many years ago and competed for the title of World Champion in chess – and even before that.

I would like to take the liberty of presenting the following request to Althingi.

For the past 6 months I have been forcibly and illegally imprisoned in Japan on the completely false and ludicrous grounds that I entered Japan on April 15, 2004 and that I 'departed' or attempted to depart Japan on July 13, 2004 with an invalid passport.

During this period my health has steadily deteriorated. I've been dizzy all of the time for about the past 2 months now. Incidentally, it's been very carefully blacked out in the press but it just so happens that I'm the very oldest prisoner here in the East Japan Immigration Detention Center. Not to mention the fact that when the Narita Airport Immigration Security authorities brutally and violently 'arrested' me (actually it was nothing but a kidnapping and everybody knows it) I was seriously injured and very nearly killed. Furthermore it is surely not beneficial to my health either physically or psychologically that they've dragged me here to Ushiku which is only about 66 kilometers from the leaking Tokaimura nuclear power plant (Japan's Chernobyl!) in Tokyo City. They just had another nuclear accident there on October 14, 2004!

And now, unfortunately, the Icelandic authorities' recent offer of residence and of entry to Iceland without a passport has not sufficed to prompt the hard-headed and hard-hearted Japanese authorities/kidnappers to let me go to your excellent country.

In case you're wondering why I have no U.S. passport it's because within 24 hours of 'arresting' me the U.S. and Japanese authorities working in collusion illegally confiscated and physically destroyed my perfectly valid U.S. passport # 27792702!

Neither the Japanese nor the American authorities have ever bothered to offer any explanation or justification whatsoever for this outrageous criminal act. Apparently they're strictly heeding Disraeli's advice which was to: 'Never apologize, never explain!'

Because of all the foregoing I would therefore like to formally request that Althingi grant me Icelandic citizenship so that I may actually enjoy the offer of residence in Iceland that your Minister for Foreign Affairs Mr. David Oddsson has so graciously extended to me.
Most respectfully
Bobby Fischer

Three days later, on the 22nd of January 2005, the decision to grant Bobby Fischer a residence permit received a harsh blow when the Japanese Justice Ministry lawyers said they were not prepared to change Fischer's deportation destination to Iceland, and that he would have to remain in detention. Bobby's lawyer Masako Suzuki reacted by stating that it was against international law to keep him detained and that Japan's Ministry of Justice was violating international law.

A residence permit was not sufficient. This meant that the matter might have to be pursued through the Icelandic parliament or the government. Within the group there was no consensus about what do to next. We had fought for Bobby's release, but Gudfridur Lilja Gretarsdottir, the president of the Icelandic Chess Federation, and Hrafn Jökulsson were of the opinion that a certain closure had been reached in the case and parted with us.

For the other members of the group that later was named the RJF group, Gudmundur Thorarinsson, Einar Einarsson, Gardar Sverrison, Magnus Skulason, Ingvar Asmundsson, Saemi Palsson and me, it seemed that the only natural option was to fight on. A trip to Japan was planned, but now all of a sudden there were some newcomers on the boat. I welcomed the idea that an old friend of mine, Pall Magnusson, would cover the issue for Channel 2, but there were others, too. Fridrik Gudmundsson was a filmmaker who wanted to make a documentary, and Kristinn Hrafnsson was now working independently, but for many years had been on the team of RUV, the Icelandic National Broadcasting Service, as a reporter, and later was with Channel 2.

Pall Magnusson had been a key figure in organizing the chess World Cup tournaments in 1988 and 1991 in Reykjavik. He had got to know the likes of Garry Kasparov, Anatoly Karpov, Boris Spassky, Mikhail Tal, Viktor Kortchnoi, Jan Timman, Nigel Short and Lajos Portisch. From his perspective the missing link was Bobby Fischer. With the full support of Saemi Palsson they were planning to make a documentary about Bobby and his friendship with Saemi.

Einar Einarsson, Gudmundur Thorarinsson and Gardar Sverrisson also went to Japan. It was quite a delegation. Going to Japan was a costly undertaking, but Einar had managed to raise some funds. Before the trip the Icelandic government issued a special passport for Bobby Fischer. I had some other obligations, so I didn't go, but I was sure that the trip would be a success and that Gudmundur Thorarinsson's experience as a former member of the Icelandic parliament would be valuable. Saemi told me that Bobby wanted some reading material and before he flew to Japan I handed him three books from my own library: *Capablanca*, by Edward Winter, *Soviet Chess* by Andrew Soltis, and *Alekhine, Agony of a Chess Genius* by Pablo Moran.

In Tokyo the group met John Bosnitch, a Canadian journalist of Serbian descent and a political activist, and Bobby's lawyer, Masako Suzuki. At times the relations within the group were strained. At the press conference an argument broke out which raised the interest of the media people. The group's main success was that it managed to elevate Fischer's case to the floor of the Japanese parliament. There some discussions took place, without any conclusion. The international media kept track of events and finally it was the Icelandic parliament's turn to clear the road for Bobby's freedom.

On the 21st of March 2005 the Icelandic parliament, the Althingi, decided to grant Bobby Fischer Icelandic citizenship. By a special variation from the usual protocol, the measure was pushed through in only 12 minutes. No one opposed it. Of the 63 members of parliament 40 were in favour, there were 2 abstentions, and 21 members were absent.

Chapter Seven

Illugi said, 'Grey-belly's knocking at the door, brother.'
'And knocks hard too,' said Grettir, 'and ruthlessly', and at that moment the door burst open.
Grettir's Saga

I am not in the habit of keeping a diary, but on special occasions I tend to make notes. On the 24th of March 2005, I wrote: 'A plane is closing in on Reykjavik airport. A man who once had a day named after him in New York and was given the key to the city gate by its Mayor, is now, according to a U.S. state department spokesman, a fugitive from justice. There is a strong sense of drama and everyone witnessing the plane touch ground late in the evening is overwhelmed by the historical significance of the moment.'

At the moment the plane landed, I was standing on the roof of one of the airport buildings giving a live interview to RUV, the state-run television. For the journalist interviewing me the arrival of the plane was the moment to abruptly break off the interview, ignoring the fact that we were on air.

On the tarmac a gathering of about 200 youngsters was waiting. They were holding welcome signs, clapping their hands and chanting 'Bobby, Bobby Fischer' over and over again. After a while the doors opened and Bobby Fischer stepped out of the chartered plane. An flight attendant helped him out and his first steps on Icelandic ground seemed somewhat shaky. He was dressed in baggy blue jeans, a light blue denim shirt and a sweater. There had not been time for a haircut, which was badly needed after nine months in Japanese detention. To me the bushy-bearded man very much looked like a man from the mountains.

I had driven from my home in Kopavogur, Iceland's second biggest city south of Reykjavik, down to Reykjavik airport not knowing what to expect. Because of foggy conditions in Copenhagen the group had driven to an airport in southern Sweden, from where they flew to Iceland in a private jet owned by the largest privately-owned Icelandic company, the Baugur Group. To my mind this showed an incredible and simply unbelievable lack of judgement on the part of my old friend Pall Magnusson, news anchorman at the commercial station Channel 2 and head of the news department. His action put the independence of Channel 2's news reporting into question. Which was sad, as in Iceland Magnusson was sometimes referred to as the most trusted man on TV.

The plane was carrying Bobby Fischer, his partner Miyoko Watai, Saemundur Palsson, Fridrik Gudmundsson, Kristinn Hrafnsson, Pall Magnusson, a flight attendant and the pilots. Fridrik Gudmundsson would later emerge as the director of the documentary Me & Bobby Fischer with Kristinn Hrafnsson co-writing the script. Pall was there in a dual role. His official status was head of the Channel 2 news department, but Fridrik had also asked him to be the narrator of the documentary, a role he would later decline to take on.

When the plane touched ground in Reykjvik, Pall managed to block all access for the assembled international media. His personal intentions also crossed the plans of Einar Einarsson, who on behalf of the RJF Committee was waiting to hand Fischer a letter of citizenship. In an almost surreal act, Fischer was whisked past Einar to a waiting car, and none of the RJF Committee members were allowed to shake his hand.

Bobby was driven around for some time, while most of the people who had been at the airport left. In the car, the Channel 2 film crew tried to interview him, but nothing came out of these attempts except for some ramblings about a CIA plot.

Meanwhile, police chief Geir Jon Thorisson informed us that later on we could meet Bobby at the Hotel Loftleidir. I was very frustrated by Channel 2's conduct and exchanged some very harsh words with Pall Magnusson when I met him at the Loftleidir. We shouted at each other for a few minutes. He seemed to believe Channel 2 had scored an important PR victory. I then left the hotel, as I was in no mood to meet Bobby there. Before I left I saw him coming down to greet Ingvar, Einar, Gudmundur, Gardar and Magnus. After a pleasant chat Bobby retired with Miyoko to suite 470, the same suite he had been living in during the match with Spassky in 1972.

The following day Einar Einarsson delivered the following press announcement on behalf of the RJF Committee:

'As your reporters and other spectators noticed, the reception ceremony for the arrival of Bobby Fischer and his fiancée, Miyoko Watai, unfortunately careened out of control due to the interference of the Channel 2 news editor, Pall Magnusson. Parties on behalf of Channel 2 covered the expense of the private jet that brought Fischer to Iceland. It must be utterly unprecedented that a member of the press should take such an affair out of the hands of the organizers and steer the course of events in order to monopolize press coverage of it. Fischer was told to stride right by his supporters in the reception committee and straight to a car that stood at the ready, not far from the plane, so that other reporters, photographers, and television stations were able to take very few pictures of him as he stepped onto Icelandic soil. He and his party were then driven away and taken on a short drive through the neighbourhood.

Ranking police officer Geir Jon Thorisson and his staff had roped off the reception area with yellow tape and had made all the necessary preparations so that the reception would go smoothly. But then, when the plane had landed, everything took a different course than expected because Geir Jon misunderstood the situation and took orders from the news editor of Channel 2 (the underwriters of the flight) and not from the RJF Committee, which had worked to free Fischer and had arranged both for his coming to the country and for a small reception without speeches.

After having boarded the plane with the customs officers, Geir Jon returned with the message that Fischer was so exhausted that he didn't feel up to shaking the hands of the seven of us who were waiting to welcome him. And there would be no interviews. Then, when Fischer disembarked from the plane, who else but a Channel 2 reporter comes charging forth, right past the police and straight up to Fischer, and begins asking the 'exhausted' traveller questions. When that happened, the well-organized reception plans dissolved into chaos. More people ran into the roped-off area, and soon the police couldn't control the crowd. The reception committee had planned to present Fischer with his Letter of Citizenship, as symbolic testimony to his having become an Icelander, but this couldn't be accomplished and will have to wait for a better time.

The message was sent to us supporters that Fischer would return and would arrive at Hotel Loftleidir in 15-20 minutes, whereupon the reception committee could see him. This did indeed happen. The reporters from Channel 2, who had virtually kidnapped Fischer for a short time, returned with him to the plane and interviewed and filmed him again with the jet in the background. They were the only news crew to do so, as the other members of the press had packed up and left by that time. Then Fischer came, with his friend Saemundur, into Hotel Loftleidir, and greeted everyone who had been waiting for him very warmly and graciously. He was lively and energetic, and he seemed anything but exhausted. Of course he was tired by this time, however, and relieved to retire to the lovely suite that he stayed in back in 1972 so he could get some rest.'

A popular columnist, Gudmundur Steingrimsson, wrote an article in Frettabladid: 'Sometimes I get what I call a silly-shiver. It is an awkward feeling I can feel down my spine, actually quite a comfortable feeling and is usually associated with something out of the ordinary happening, when an event gets completely out of control. "Welcome to Iceland, Mr. Fischer. How does it feel to be home?" When I heard the Channel 2 reporter utter this sentence I immediately had it – this awkward feeling, forcefully and immediately!'

The Frettabladid editorial was entitled 'Channel 2's own goal', and a special mention was made of the fact that Pall Magnusson had used a company jet belonging to the Baugur Group to sponsor Bobby's flight to Iceland. The editorial ended with the line: 'An appalling lack of judgement which leaves one almost speechless.' Bobby's reception by Channel 2 is now considered to be a major flop and the people involved are still the laughing stock in Iceland.

The following day Bobby Fischer had his hair cut and held a press conference at the Hotel Loftleidir. Saemi, his body-guard of 1972, was there with him, again thrown into the spotlight. In his blunt statements Bobby addressed his usual enemies with his usual vigour. American correspondent Jeremy Schaap, the son of the late Dick Schaap, an old friend of Bobby's, explained to his audience that he was '...wondering what had become of the boy who needed the elder Schaap to take him home to Brooklyn because he could not ride alone on the subway.'

Jeremy Schaap tried his utmost to humiliate Bobby. In answer to his question Bobby said: 'He rapped me very hard, he said I don't have a sane bone in my body, I didn't forget that.' And later he addressed Schaap again and talked about his father, who once took him to Knicks games: 'His father, many many years ago, befriended me... acted kind of like a father figure, and then later, like a typical Jewish snake, he had the most vicious things to say about me.'

To which Jeremy Schaap replied, temporarily silencing Bobby: 'Honestly I don't know that you've done much here today really to disprove anything he said .'

To which Jeremy Schaap replied, temporarily silencing Bobby: 'Yes Bobby, and you've done nothing today to disprove anything my father ever said about you.'

Schaap may have had a point, but to my mind this was an attack that was not called for at that moment. It didn't seem right to have this discussion with a man who has just been released from prison after nine rough months.

A few weeks later Jeremy Schaap was rewarded for his work in Reykjavik. At the Emmys he won the Dick Schaap Award for Outstanding Writing, an award named after his father, for an *Outside the Lines* feature titled 'Finding Bobby Fischer'.

The New York Times reported about another mission shortly afterwards: '... Schaap was at a news conference promoting Mike Tyson's June 11 fight against Kevin McBride. Tyson asked him what he had been doing in Iceland. Tracking another former world champion, Schaap said.

"Bobby Fischer", Tyson said. "That guy's crazy!"'

The media coverage was almost unbelievable. Several times I was called by staff writers from the *New York Times* and other newspapers. When I looked for the name Bobby Fischer on Google it turned out that he was all over the news. The death of Pope John Paul II on April 2 certainly got more attention, but Fischer was close.

I met Bobby for the first time on Monday, March 27. According to Saemi he wanted to meet me. After his first few days in Reykjavik I was the only one of the RJF group whom Bobby had not yet seen in person. When Gudmundur Thorarinsson had been allowed to talk to Bobby in Japan he had mentioned the six lectures on Bobby Fischer's chess career that I had given on the premises of the Icelandic Chess Federation. Attendance had been surprisingly good and the audience had listened to my views and watched the games that I demonstrated with great interest. During one of the lectures I had concluded that in his chess in the early seventies Bobby Fischer had been 20 years ahead of his time, a conclusion which Gudmundur did not fail to convey to him. 'Really? Did he say that?', Bobby had said to him. It turned out that he was also pleased with the three chess books that I had given them to present to him.

I guess I had been preparing for this moment for a good part of my life. Together with Saemi I went to his suite at the Hotel Loftleidir. Miyoko came to the door and, behind her, there he was – the man. He walked over to me and we shook hands. He looked relaxed, liberated. 'I think I have seen you before', he said, 'or maybe I have seen your picture.' He was very courteous and expressed his appreciation for the work we had done to free him. Saemi nodded at much of what he was saying and sometimes he would comment, 'You're absolutely right, Bobby'. Saemi and Miyoko almost looked like a team in the way they tried to please Bobby. I was very well prepared to meet him. I had not only studied him as a chess player, but also as a person. I had no wish to discuss his favourite obsessions with him or to help him in one of his fights. My main purpose was just to have a good time with him, show him around, be a good friend.

It was mostly small talk that day. Bobby obviously loved soul music and played some music by Ricky Wilson. A huge chocolate Easter egg was on a table by the sofa in the comfortable living room. He asked about my writing skills because he was looking for someone to work with him on writing about the prearranged matches between Karpov and Kasparov. I told him that his biography and a book on his chess career would be much more interesting. He nodded in agreement, but said that his first priority was finishing a book about the prearranged matches. He told me that he thought that every World Championship match between the Soviets was prearranged move by move.

On April 2, the RJF Committee had a Welcome Bobby dinner for Bobby and Miyoko. They came with Saemi and his wife. It was very well organized by Einar Einarsson. There he finally handed Bobby the Letter of Citizenship. Several local journalists and a couple from abroad were present to witness this special moment. They left when the dinner started. The evening was a quiet and happy occasion for all of us. After dinner we all withdrew to the bar and there I spoke at length with Bobby. He told me about that stressful day, July 3, 1972, when he was in Anthony Saidy's home in New York and took a phone call from the White House. 'Mr. Bobby Fischer. This is Henry Kissinger.' Bobby imitated Kissinger's deep and slightly hoarse voice very well and we both were laughing.

Then I asked him if he had given Bill Lombardy a call. A few weeks earlier his former second had written an article supporting his case that had been published in Morgunbladid. 'Yeah, I phoned him from jail and told him to write an article', Bobby said. 'I told him that he was obliged to be of assistance. And he did it without asking any questions. Lombardy hates them even more than me', he explained. There had also been an article against Bobby, a very hostile attack, that was written by American grandmaster Ilya Gurevich. It had also appeared in Morgunbladid, but at this point I had little wish to bring it to Bobby's attention. But as I noticed later, he kept track of anything written about him and I am sure he knew about this article, too.

It was probably hard for Bobby to forget the 'select company' he had been living with for the past nine months in Japan. Quite surprisingly Bobby had nothing but admiration for the Japanese guards in the Ushiku

67

detention centre. 'I was told their wages are just horribly low, but these guys were so disciplined', he said in an admiring tone. 'A few times I and some other inmates tried to confront them with some requests or even demands, but the guards stood completely still and gave us a stony look without blinking an eye, with absolutely expressionless faces.' He revealed to me that he played some chess in there and that one of the inmates had been quite a decent chess player.

Now finally he had reached freedom's shores. Or that was what we thought or rather hoped. For a brief moment it looked as if Bobby Fischer's world was new and everything seemed possible.

Outside Hotel Holt snow was starting to fall when we were about to leave. Bobby took a seat with Miyoko in a waiting taxi. As he always did, Bobby took the front seat. He rolled down the window and we exchanged a few more words. Before he closed the window he asked for my mobile phone number and wrote it down. From then on he would start calling me on a regular basis.

Chapter Eight

'Weepest thou now, Skarphedinn?' 'Not so,' says Skarphedinn, 'but true it is that the smoke makes one's eyes smart, but is it as it seems to me, dost thou laugh?' 'So it is surely,' says Gunnar, 'and I have never laughed since thou slewest Thrain on Markfleet.'
Then Skarphedinn said — 'He now is a keepsake for thee'; and with that he took out of his purse the jaw-tooth which he had hewn out of Thrain, and threw it at Gunnar, and struck him in the eye, so that it started out and lay on his cheek.
Njal's Saga

Bobby's coming 'home' to Iceland stirred up a lot of emotions. Generally our effort was appreciated, but some were unable to forget or forgive his radio interviews. I was playing blitz on the Internet Chess Club when a player by the name of Parsifal introduced himself and expressed his disappointment about me dining with that 'arsehole', as he put it. Later he added that Bobby '...was never World Champion'. It was an old friend, English grandmaster James Plaskett. Of course he was entitled to his opinion, but I sent him an e-mail, part of which I publish here:

Dear James Plaskett,
There were many good reasons not to lend Bobby Fischer a helping hand whilst in jail in Japan, but given the strong possibility that the man was/is seriously ill was reason enough to try to help him. I will never regret that. Personally I make no distinction between, say, a schizo-paranoid, a person with cancer, a brain tumour or any other disease. Everyone should have some basic human rights. Jail was certainly not the correct place for Fischer.

It is very clear to me that if Fischer had been sent to the USA he would have died in jail. Over the years I have dined with many people I have had some mixed feelings towards. It has not bothered me so much. It goes without saying that the RJF-committee that worked so hard to bring Fischer to Iceland had to invite him to a dinner of this sort. We are now about to bring to Iceland a young lad who was left rotting in a Texas jail for 8 years since he was 13 years old, believe it or not.

I hope this e-mail finds you in good spirit and I hope I can shed some light on my stance in the matter of Bobby Fischer.

All the best, hope to see you one day,
Helgi Olafsson

The young lad we were trying to free from a Texas jail was called Aron Palmi Agustsson. It was part of our wish to make it clear that our thoughts about individual freedom did not only concern Bobby Fischer. We kept the name RJF-committee, but indicated that instead of standing for Robert James Fischer, the letters had now come to mean Rights, Justice and Freedom. To end the incredible injustice that had been done to Aron Palmi Agustsson we sent an open letter to Texas Governor Rick Perry that included the following lines: '...Aron Palmi Agustsson (...) was unfortunate enough, when only a child himself, to be sentenced for sexual harassment of a young playmate. For this fateful error in childish judgment, our young Icelandic friend was sentenced, when only 13 years old, to spend 10 years in a correctional facility in the State of Texas penal system. At this writing, he has served slightly less than 8 years of that sentence. If nothing changes in the handling of his case, he must serve just over two additional years before reclaiming his freedom.'

Paul Nikolov, who had strong ties with the weekly magazine The Reykjavik Grapevine and for some time had a seat in the Althingi, the Icelandic parliament, for the Left-Green Party, had this to say about our involvement in 2005: 'A great deal of voice was given to Agustsson, who contended that he was "just playing doctor" with the young boy, and he's had a considerable number of supporters, including the Church of Iceland who, on their website (www.kirkjan.is) called the drive to free Agustsson "a human rights battle". Yet the strongest group clamouring to free Agustsson is an organization calling itself the RJF Group. This is RJF Group's second project; their first was to free former world chess champion and raving anti-Semite Bobby Fischer from a Japanese prison and bring him to Iceland. In fact, while the group contends that "RJF" stands for "Rights, Justice and Freedom", this also happens to be the initials of Robert James Fischer, another person of questionable character that a small but loud minority was able to bring into this country, to the embarrassment of everyone else.'

One day I was driving Bobby around and we stopped at the Perlan building, a well-known sightseeing spot in Reykjavik, from where you have a good view of the city. I had a cup of coffee, Bobby had tea. He never drank coffee, but he liked tea and at his home it had struck me how lovingly Miyoko would pour him a cup of tea, sometimes with lemon. He once told me that during his first trip to Argentina in 1959 he had been given a cup of special Argentinian coffee. The brand was so strong that it had an almost immediate effect. It felt great. In fact it felt so great that it had made him wary. If it was so good, there inevitably had to be a downside, and he decided not to drink coffee anymore.

While he was drinking his tea at Perlan, Einar Einarsson called me about a RJF Committee meeting at his home later that day. I asked Bobby whether he would like to join us and so he did. He came to at least one more meeting. Bobby's input at the meetings he attended was mostly about how the system in states like Texas worked. 'Of course this young boy is in dire need of counselling, but to put him away for 10 years is simply outrageous', he said.

The fact of the matter is that we were simply petitioning with the boy's family to have him serve the rest of his sentence in Iceland. In the end Aron Palmi served his full sentence, 10 years, in Texas, but the RJF Committee supported him financially as well as mentally during this time. Shortly after his return to Iceland in the autumn of 2007 he published a book about his life in the juvenile detention facility, *I Can't Let Them See Me Cry*, which he co-wrote with Icelandic journalist Jon Trausti Reynisson.

During his first weeks in Iceland Bobby lived in his old suite at the Hotel Loftleidir. He did not seem to mind that he was charged between $250 and $300 per day. During his time in Iceland Bobby was living off his earnings from the 1992 match with Spassky and had no financial problems. Nevertheless I contacted the hotel manager and complained about the steep price. The rate was then lowered considerably and Bobby was happy about this initiative of mine he had not even asked for.

I felt it was my duty to drive him around from time to time and dine with him in restaurants. On several occasions we went to the cinema. The first film we went to see together was called *Maria Full of Grace*. It was shown at a Reykjavik film festival. I had made an appointment with Bobby. He had told me that I could find him near a bookstore in the city centre. I went there together with a friend of mine, but when we got there Bobby was nowhere in sight. Then someone pointed out a person who was sitting at a bench nearby. It was Bobby. I introduced him to my friend and then we drove to the cinema. Later I found out that he utterly disliked films without 'substance' as he put it, films without a clear plot. The film festival's focus was on films from Latin America. This one had some Catholic overtones and as it turned out Bobby was sympathetic towards the Catholic church. Unfortunately this sympathy was mainly connected to certain anti-Semitic tendencies in the Catholic church.

As we were walking there at a fast pace, Bobby indicated that he wanted to be in the cinema exactly at the moment when the film began, but I told him there was no need to hurry.

'Are you sure we won't be late?' he asked.

'I am pretty sure', I answered.

'Pretty sure is not good enough, Helgi', he responded.

We made the start of the film just in time and Bobby took a seat in the back row. The narrative revolved around a young woman who decides to take a life-threatening trip from Columbia to New York, acting as a mule for a drug lord carrying cocaine in her belly. At the end of the film Bobby commented on the exploitation of the poor people in Columbia.

The other RJF Committee members, Saemi Palsson, Einar Einarsson and Gardar Sverrisson helped in many practical matters. Bobby's typical wishes could lead to amusing situations. When he opened a bank account in one of the Icelandic banks he asked for an old-fashioned customer book with the status of his invoices printed in it. The bank was actually prepared for such requests, an old typewriter was brought out and Bobby got his way.

At this time he was still looking for a suitable flat and I went with him to several places in Reykjavik. He told me the area outside the Hotel Loftleidir was becoming very noisy and he had difficulties with his sleep. Sometimes Einar was with us. Bobby was very fond of the old houses in 101 Reykjavik, as the old part of the city is known. The thick concrete walls seemed to have special appeal to him. 'Solid walls,' he said, 'just like my chess.'

I tried to explain to him that the old part of Reykjavik was also a magnet for all sorts of delinquents. Moreover, the whole area is the scene of Reykjavik's notorious nightlife, not a place for someone trying to find peace and quiet.

We also checked a few guesthouses. Later I realized that he was trying to find a place for his alleged Filipino child Jinky Young and her mother Marilyn Young. As I learned from Saemi they were expected to be in Iceland in September of that year.

Finally, in mid-summer, Bobby moved to Klapparstigur 5 in 101 Reykjavik. The enormous modern white building is situated by the sea. I think Saemi knew the owner. His flat was on the fourth floor with a lift inside the huge building. The apartment he leased was completely furnished. Such flats are quite expensive and luxurious and seldom available for rent. Earlier on Einar and I had shown him another spacious flat in the same building complex. The owner ran a successful real estate company together with Icelandic grandmaster Gudmundur Sigurjonsson and he was ready to rent it to Bobby. However, for some reason Bobby did not like the flat, even though it was better than the one Saemi later found for him. In any case we were happy that he was out of the Hotel Loftleidir. The apartment was within walking distance from Bokin, an old second-hand bookstore he started to visit on a daily basis.

In May 2005 Miyoko was again in town and the three of us had lunch at Bobby's favourite vegetarian restaurant, A Naestu Grösum (literally 'the next grass', a jocular reference to the mockery that the first vegetarians in Iceland invoked), on the corner of Klapparstigur and Laugavegur, the main shopping street in central Reykjavik. Once again the 'prearranged games' between Karpov and Kasparov in the 1984/85 match were on the agenda. According to Bobby the ninth game, won by Karpov mainly because of an incredible knight retreat on move 46, was more or less based on his win against Anthony Saidy from the U.S. Championship 1963/64, the legendary championship that he won with a perfect 11/11 score. 'There is absolutely no chance they could have reached this position without prior knowledge of my win', he stated. I did not give much credence to such views. 'It seems a pretty casual position to me. This pawn formation has occurred many times I am sure', I said, and then even dared to change the subject. Bobby looked at me in bewilderment. 'No way', he shot back. 'I am absolutely sure you could not find a single example of such a position, at least not before my game with Saidy', he said in a very forceful manner.

Eager to prove him wrong, the same day I contacted Dadi Jonsson, a chess columnist, the former chairman of the Reykjavik chess club Hellir, and a computer scientist. I told him about the conversation I had had with Bobby and asked him to find a similar position, especially one before the Saidy game.

Both in Bobby's game against Saidy and in the Karpov-Kasparov game each side had six pawns, spread over two wings, while the suffering side had a slightly restricted bishop that had to fight against the opponent's superior knight. In both games the knight triumphed and the win was achieved in similar fashion. Dadi set to work with the help of the database of the Chess Assistant program that contained three million games. First he created a smaller database of 20,000 games in which both sides had six pawns and one of them had a knight and the other a bishop. Next he refined his search to find games with the exact characteristics he was looking for. The harvest consisted of 14 games that were played before Saidy-Fischer. From these, four had ended in a draw, others were trivial wins and some were badly played. At this point Dadi began to think that Bobby might be right after all. Maybe he had been the first to show how to win this position, since the winning method was far from trivial. But then he found the game Levenfish-Kotov, played in Leningrad in 1939, which Levenfish won using a method similar to the way Fischer beat Saidy. The same went for a game Fairhurst-Keres, played in Hastings in 1955.

Dadi brought me the complete print-out consisting of several hundred pages and I took them to Bobby's suite in Loftleidir. He was impressed. Looking through the games he laughed: 'Unbelievable! Wow, great research.'

Six months later he tried to discuss the prearrangements again with me while I was driving him around in my car. Keeping a straight face I reminded him of our discussion of the Saidy game. 'But that was only one example', he objected, slightly offended. I smiled a bit and we drove on.

It was nearly impossible to talk to Fischer about chess without going into the 'prearrangements'. He was also of the opinion that Kasparov's win over Topalov in the Wijk aan Zee tournament of 1999, arguably the most spectacular game of the last decade of the twentieth century, was all prearranged. 'I have never played a game like this', he said.

We had an interesting discussion, though, about the 11th match game of the 1972 match, in which Spassky, playing the white pieces, played the stunning novelty 14.♘b1!!. Confused by this thunderbolt, Bobby went astray with his 15th move and lost in only 31 moves. Eleven years later, at an international tournament in Hanover, Anatoly Karpov, the then world champion, reached the same position against Jingchuan Qi from China. On his 15th move Karpov simply withdrew his knight to e7 and won convincingly. We pondered this position for a while and then Bobby all of a sudden concluded: 'Black is winning.' A curious statement about such a complex position. With his pawn capture on move 8 Black had severely damaged White's pawn structure, and Bobby probably felt that if White could not make any serious headway after this concession, he would gradually lose the ensuing battle.

I was surprised when at that point he told me that he had been afraid of the Russians and that he was sure that the stunning novelty with which Spassky had surprised him in that game was an improvement cooked up specially for this game by Spassky's team. Perhaps it was, perhaps it wasn't. Spassky, in any case, has stated more than once that this idea came to him over the board.

Chapter Nine

After that they fare to the Point, and two ravens flew along with them all the way.
Njal's Saga

In early May of 2005, when Bobby was still living in the suite at the Hotel Loftleidir, I got a phone call from Joel Lautier, then president of the ACP, the Association of Chess Professionals. He told me his plans to come to Iceland accompanied by Boris Spassky and a man I had never heard about before in chess circles, Alex Titomirov. Bobby asked me to make a quick check on Titomirov on Google, which I did.

He seemed to be a Russian expatriate living in Paris. I did not exclude the possibility that he had suffered when the dot-com bubble burst. A revelation to us concerned some highly controversial deals he had made in the past. 'The genetic software goose has laid golden eggs for its insiders', ran one line on Google about Titomirov's exit package from a company called InforMax Inc. 'This guy might be desperate', Bobby said to me.

I pointed out that there was a strong likelihood that support came from a wealthy Syrian lady living in Paris, Nahed Ojjeh. She had been an important benefactor of French chess, had vowed in 2002 to work on the reunification of the chess world, which at the time had two rival world championships, and was clearly backing Joel Lautier as president of the ACP.

An article in *The Independent* titled 'City mystery as chess queen challenges media knight in bid war battle' revealed the following: 'On her website, entitled "Who is Nadeh Ojjeh?", she talks gushingly about her ambition to take chess to the masses, championing its teaching in schools so the West can rival the chess masters of the East. She liked the game so much she bought a Paris chess club and tried to set up a new world chess championship. But she fell out with the British media company the Einstein Group, over sponsorship.'

In any case Bobby was eager to meet Boris and saw no problem with shaking hands with Joel Lautier. 'Of course I will meet some chess players', he said. Their arrival in Iceland shortly after Bobby's escape from Japan naturally attracted a lot of attention. However, all efforts to photograph Bobby and Boris together failed. I was alone with Bobby in his suite when Boris came to meet him. I felt slightly uncomfortable in the room, so I left them alone. It was like brothers were finally meeting after a very long time. Boris hugged him and Bobby responded to the hug, slightly clumsily, not completely comfortable. They hadn't seen each other since 1994.

Bobby didn't seem to mind having a meeting with Titomirov, and a few hours later the following people assembled in Bobby's suite: Bobby Fischer, Boris Spassky, Alex Titomirov, Joel Lautier, Einar Einarsson and me. There Titomirov outlined his plans for a Bobby Fischer match. He started by insulting Boris Spassky by stating that it would be pointless to stage a third match between them. Some other top-class grandmaster had to play Bobby, preferably World Champion Vladimir Kramnik.

According to Titomirov the live games would be broadcast to a worldwide audience via the Internet and people would pay an admission fee for the whole event. Titomirov expected to raise millions of dollars with this business idea. Anyone who would dare to broadcast the match without a licence would immediately be sued.

Later that evening there was a dinner at the Hotel Holt with Boris, Joel, Einar and Titomirov. I could sense that Spassky was far from happy about this trip. The next morning they all left for Paris. Titomirov's other ideas concerning a Bobby Fischer match against a Chinese female player failed to impress Bobby. It seems to me now that it was very important for Titomirov to have Bobby's signature on a declaration of goodwill and that the 'mysterious' lady Madame Nahed Ojjeh would finance any project Bobby was willing to participate in. Later that summer Joel Lautier called me and informed me that Kramnik was interested in coming to Iceland. But he never showed up.

Spassky's next visit to Iceland coincided with a happier occasion. On February 11, 2006, Gudfridur Lilja Gretarsdottir, the president of the Icelandic Chess Federation, organized a special programme in the headquarters of Landsbankinn in honour of Iceland's first grandmaster, Fridrik Olafsson, who had turned 70 on January 26, 2005.

The speakers in front of a full house were Boris Spassky, Gudmundur Thorarinsson, PM Halldor Blöndal and me. Earlier that day I had met Spassky in his hotel and gave him a book of Fridrik's collected games. He decided to demonstrate a very fine game that Fridrik won against Efim Geller in the Bled tournament in 1961. Afterwards Boris and Fridrik played a few rapid exhibition games on the board on which Spassky had played his match with Bobby in 1972.

I picked Fridrik's highly interesting but far from flawless victory over Tukmakov at the 4th Reykjavik international tournament in 1972. Gudmundur talked at length about Fridrik's chess career and his everlasting fight with the chess clock, and compared his international status to that of pop star Björk. Halldor Blöndal, who had worked closely with Fridrik in the Icelandic parliament where Fridrik held the post of General Secretary for over 20 years, dealt with stories from his glory days, especially from the time he played in the Portoroz Interzonal in 1958.

Fridrik had decided to invite Bobby, Boris and his wife Marina, and me for a lunch the following day. He asked me to make arrangements. I phoned an old friend, Hermann Gunnarsson, a former football star, TV and radio host, and asked for help in this matter. His son Hendrik is a well-known chef and at the time he was running a restaurant called Skolabru, very close to the parliament square. Hendrik understood the situation and generously offered to open the restaurant only for us. We were supposed to be there at 1 pm and I was going to pick up Bobby. When I came to his flat I told him where we were going.

'Out of the question. The press is going to be there. We will go to a place of my choice', he said. I explained to him that it was Fridrik who was inviting us for lunch and orders had to be made well in advance. 'It's my way or no way', he continued in his stubborn manner.

I suggested various ways to smuggle him into the restaurant, but he did not give in. 'Tell them to come over and from here we will decide', he said. There was no point arguing, so I told him I would drive to the restaurant. When I got there Fridrik, Boris and their wives had already ordered some drinks. 'I am sorry, but Bobby refuses to come with me', I said.

Neither Fridrik nor Boris seemed too surprised. Fridrik suggested that Boris would telephone Bobby and so he did. 'Bobby, what shall be our next move?' was Spassky's first sentence.

I could not hear his answer but it was decided that I, together with Boris, would go to Bobby's flat and try to persuade him to come over to the restaurant. Spassky had not been to Bobby's place before. 'Bobby, this is a very good flat', Spassky said. He started to walk around, casting an appreciative look at what he saw. Without any real reason he turned to me and in passing said, 'So you are the ambassador of Bobby Fischer in Iceland?' Then he approached Bobby and, like a dentist, he asked him to open his mouth. 'Let me see your teeth', he said, standing close to him. Many years before Bobby had the fillings of his teeth removed. He felt that the fillings irritated the gum and feared a toxic effect. This was the reason and not the story cooked up by a journalist that 'the Russians' might be sending radio signals to the fillings. Bobby had not been to a dentist for a long time and it showed. He had lost a few teeth and those remaining had decayed. Even so there was no real bad breath noticeable. Spassky was very insistent and Bobby indeed opened his mouth. Then he said, which I regarded as a flat denial: 'They are OK.'

Now we had to solve the issue about the restaurant. Bobby had already 'won' by getting Boris to come over, so I suggested an alternative route to the restaurant. We would drive around downtown Reykjavik, and as the street facing the Skolabru was an open area, any journalist would be spotted immediately. Hesitantly Bobby agreed on this and I was about to open the door of his flat when he urged me and Spassky to take care: 'Someone might be standing at that floor.'

Very carefully we left the flat, then we took the lift, but when the door opened on the first floor there were a number of people waiting on the first floor. The sudden appearance of two world chess champions in the midst of what seemed like a family gathering raised some eyebrows, but I almost burst out laughing because Bobby had taken such careful steps to avoid meeting anyone.

There was nothing else to do but drive towards the Skolabru, and to ensure that no member of the press was in sight. Spassky got out literally on the doorstep of the restaurant and I circled in the car with Bobby before I finally found a parking place about 100 metres away. While I parked the car, Bobby went to the restaurant. There he was received by Boris, who put on a great act. Talking to Bobby he went around the restaurant, opening doors here and there and pushing aside curtains, saying, see, Bobby, there is no one here, no journalists, nothing. Bobby followed him move around and then smiled to everyone's relief.

Bobby ordered a beer and shook hands with Spassky's wife Marina, Fridrik and his wife Audur. Then he turned to Fridrik and said: 'We had a beautiful game.' But it stopped there, with no elaborations or his repeated 'chess is dead' mantra.

During dinner Bobby and Boris discussed some games from the '72 match. 'Some of your moves Boris were really terrible', Bobby said, and pointed out specially the horrific blunder in the 14th game, when with an unexplainable pawn push on move 27 he threw away his winning chances in a highly promising position. Then the conversation touched on some of the disputes. Surprisingly Bobby told everybody how embarrassed he had been on Spassky's behalf by Geller's statement to the press before the 17th game. Claiming that electronic devices and chemical substances were playing a role in the match, he had the light fixture and the chairs subjected to a thorough examination.

Bobby was happy with the dinner. Afterwards Marina asked for permission to photograph him outside the restaurant with her husband, but Bobby objected. Then everyone went home. Around midnight he called me and started the conversation by insisting that the waiter was most probably a CIA rat. He said this man had also been working at the Hotel Loftleidir. But he was laughing and I did not take him seriously.

A few days later I received the following e-mail from Spassky:

Dear Helgi,
Thank you once more for the book of Fridrik's games. It was funny for me to see how you deal with Bobby. He can torture everybody. Thanks for the nice lunch.

Let's be in touch.
Boris Spassky

Chapter Ten

... but the next summer he was late 'boun'; and men told him that his ship was not seaworthy.
Flosi said she was quite good enough for an old and death-doomed man, and bore his goods on
shipboard and put out to sea. But of that ship no tidings were ever heard.
Njal's saga

In 1988 Bobby Fischer had obtained U.S. Patent No. 4,884,255 for a new type of digital chess clock. Fischer's digital clock gave each player a fixed period of time at the start of the game and then added a small amount of time after each move.

The patent application filed for the invention provided this summary:

'A game timing apparatus and method for simultaneously timing events for two players is disclosed. The method involves presetting a pair of clocks for respective initial time periods, starting one of the clocks to time a first player's move, simultaneously stopping one clock and starting the other, and incrementing or decrementing each of the clocks by a time interval once for each move or a group of moves. The apparatus includes a pair of clock means, a pair of start switches for starting and stopping the clock means, and a compensation means for incrementing or decrementing each clock means by a time interval.'

The 'Fischer Clock' was an instant success. It is no exaggeration to say that the idea of having a time increment per move has revolutionized the chess world and it is now being used everywhere, from chess clubs and the Internet to all major tournaments. The basic idea is that it is more 'honest'. Instead of suddenly running out of time, as was the case with the old clocks, you always have some time to make a move. The new clock was first used when Bobby played the return match with Spassky in Sveti Stefan and Belgrade in 1992. There the rules stipulated that each player began with 111 minutes and received one minute for every move played. This meant that after 40 moves each player had been allotted 151 minutes for the first 40 moves. Before this match Bobby had played ten training games with Svetozar Gligoric, in which the time limit was 50 minutes for the entire game and one minute was added after each move. After the Fischer clock became a worldwide success, some people claimed it was nothing new, often referring to an old idea of Bronstein's. His idea had been, and it was now supported by, amongst others, Garry Kasparov, that you would get extra time after you made a move, but that you could not save up time. From a certain point onwards you would only have the extra time allotted after you pushed the clock. However, Bronstein's idea was never used.

Given the universal appeal of his clock it was tragic that Bobby never profited from his invention financially. I asked him once if it had earned him any money and he said in a matter-of-fact way: 'No.' On his arrival in Iceland a reporter asked Bobby how he intended to occupy his time in Iceland. Bobby answered that he had been working on a new chess clock, but the kidnapping had delayed those plans.

This new clock, an improved version of the one used in the 1992 match which he hoped to market, was shrouded in mystery. I doubt that Bobby had it with him when he arrived in Iceland. Most probably Miyoko brought it on one of her later visits.

I never asked him about the technical features, but he kept it on the kitchen table in the living room at Klapparstigur 5. It was huge – larger than a laptop – with more than 20 switches. I heard that Bobby had to pay the Japanese company Seiko a huge amount of money to make it, but he had hopes that Seiko would further develop the clock and then produce and market it under its brand name. While Bobby was in the detention centre Seiko rejected any such proposals. It was difficult for Bobby to understand or comprehend that big companies like Seiko could not be associated with a high-profile individual like Bobby Fischer, who on several occasions had literally gone amok in his public appearances.

I usually reserved Fridays for Bobby. Around 4 pm I would go and see him. That's what I also did on Friday, August 19, 2005. I had just finished a round of golf and felt very energetic. I drove to Klapparstigur and went through the usual routine. I called him on the ground floor, and after I had announced that it was me, he let me into the building to go up to his floor. There, as he had instructed me, I knocked on his front door. As if I were a total stranger he asked through the door: 'Who is it?' And after I had said 'It is me, Helgi', Bobby opened the door wearing a T-shirt.

'We must try the chess clock', Bobby said as I entered his flat. He brought out a chess set someone had given him. These were nothing like the quality chess pieces the young Bobby Fischer had carried with him, but were good enough for a few games of blitz.

I took a seat, in a slightly uncomfortable pose, squeezed between the table and the window in the small kitchen. There was room to move his chair back and move the table so that I would have more space, and I might have asked him to do that, but I knew that he was so concerned about the clock that he would have been reluctant to move the table. He looked after the clock with extreme care and mostly covered it with a towel to protect it against particles in the air. He sometimes indicated particles he saw on the floor and was always complaining about pollution.

Bobby had set up the pieces in their 'classical' starting position and I was hoping he would not propose a game of Fischer-Random, since I had never ever played that version of chess. Bobby had talked of an initiative in Germany to popularize the game, '...but they call it Chess960, not Fischer-Random', he said. 'They believe my image is so bad that they have given it another name.' Then he turned his attention to the clock. This monster clock was a strangely old-fashioned piece of equipment and reminded me of a control board from an old science fiction movie about nuclear war.

'Helgi, do you want a male voice or a soft female voice?' Bobby asked me. 'What do we need the voices for?' I asked back. 'The voices will warn you if your time is running out', Bobby said. 'Are there any other options?' I asked.

'Yes, there are,' Bobby said, 'but I am not sure how to activate them.'

'All right then. I think I will go for the soft female voice', I answered. Bobby set the time control at three minutes for 30 moves and thereafter three seconds would be added to every move. A very stiff time control for someone who had never played Fischer-Random. Bobby got up and returned to the kitchen table with a new item, a small cube. On top of it there was a button.

'I had this made in Belgrade', he said. Now he pushed the button and on a very small screen there appeared one of the 960 possible starting positions of Fischer-Random.

'It is absolutely random', he said. 'The position can never appear in any special order. There is no rule.'

We set up the pieces and I knew it was pointless to suggest the normal starting position. I was immediately very concentrated. Here I was sitting facing Bobby Fischer in a game of chess. The circumstances were very different from those I had dreamt of when I was a young boy. We were alone in his flat on the fourth floor at Klapparstigur 5 in Reykjavik. Not a single soul present besides the two of us. It was very quiet inside with some light traffic noises coming from a nearby street. I had never asked Bobby for a game of chess. And here he was offering me the chance to play him.

The first game I surprisingly won rather easily. One moment from this game stays in my mind – when I captured Bobby's knight on b6 with my bishop from its starting position on g1 he looked surprised. 'What's this?' he said. I was giving up a bishop for a knight. Among the many chess players I have met there is one I hold in high regard for his keen understanding of the meaningful transition when a knight is exchanged for a bishop. At that point I thought of Artur Yusupov. I have played over the games of chess legends of all times, but in this very special field Artur Yusupov really elevated the game of chess.

The capture was followed by my moving a knight to c4 and soon thereafter this knight wrecked Bobby's position from the d6 square. When he resigned Bobby swept the pieces into the centre of the board.

Before we started I had warned Bobby that I was a strong blitz player. He did not see how good I was in the second game because for some stupid reason I overlooked a bishop capturing a pawn on c5. I was fighting a pawn down with the clock ticking, but even though there were some swindling chances in the position I was sure that Bobby would see through them all.

Then all of a sudden I felt an enormous pain in my right calf. As is my habit, I had ignored the necessity of performing a stretching exercise after playing golf and now I rose to my feet screaming in great pain. Bobby jumped up from his seat. 'Hey, what's the matter?' he exclaimed. 'A terrible muscle spasm', I said.

Certainly not intentionally, this actually did seem to lull Bobby's attention when we resumed play. He somewhat carelessly made a move and fell into a trap that included a pin on his queen on c4. There was a king on a2. He shook his head. 'Shit, I must get some herring', he said. He now walked the kitchen floor like a caged lion, opened the refrigerator, grabbed a can of herring from it, poured himself a glass of orange juice, ate and drank swiftly and then returned to the board.

In the third game I was White. The position took the form of a Hedgehog with Bobby's pawns on c5 and e5, but he withdrew his forces and I had some threats with a knight on f5. Now I could well feel his strength, but I noticed that in every game he tried to castle as soon as possible. After some mistakes on my part with the limited time, Fischer got the upper hand and won with powerful chess. I remember that at one point he 'shot' his bishop from g7 to h6. Then he won another game from a drawn rook ending and in the fifth and sixth games I overstepped the time.

I regarded these games as unfinished, but Bobby of course claimed the points. Even though I can play blitz extremely fast, the time-limit Bobby offered was very difficult for me as Fischer-Random was in fact terra incognita for me. And the 'lady in the background', the soft female voice, didn't help at all. On the contrary, the voice was disturbing when time was running out.

We had an interesting argument about the final position in both games which were unfinished when I overstepped. I would have liked to play these positions. I felt I was slightly better in one position, an opinion Bobby opposed, but the other was drawish. Still, with every game he was clearly gaining in strength. He was very strong and I could sense by his mere presence the terrifying influence he must have had on his opponents in his prime.

It almost felt like the game of chess was too easy for him. His calculating abilities were great. It is difficult to describe this but it seemed that he somehow had a different calculating method than most chess players. As if he was visualizing the geography on the chessboard, and every square was somehow within his grasp. As if he had created an internal spatial map in his brain. The main thing, however, was that he was happy playing chess, as if he was finally speaking his native language.

Then after game six I had to leave. I could have played a couple more games, but at the same time I felt exhausted, drained.

'Let's play some games later', Bobby said as I opened the door. 'Any time', I answered as I left.

Those six games we played were stored in my brain for a few days and I thought about writing down all the moves. Even though each starting position was different from the others it was not such a difficult task. But Bobby had asked me to play those games to test his clock, and that being the main purpose of our match, I felt I would somehow betray him by doing so.

We did not play a single game of Fischer-Random again and I was never quite sure whether Bobby was entirely satisfied with the shuffling of the pieces. The 'classical' starting position is very harmonious and when you play the random version I felt the positions tend to lead to wing games. You are developing your bishops all the time and the battle becomes rather slow and consequently dynamism is lost.

One wonders how he would have fared had he been able to start his career playing Fischer-Random. I am not sure. Bobby Fischer was lucky in his chess in the sense that he had met the best and the brightest when he was only 15 years old at his first international appearance in the Portoroz

Interzonal in 1958. Mikhail Tal especially had a profound influence on him. It took him some time, but Bobby found his style, which is very important for every chess player. I am not sure he could have developed such a powerful arsenal of weapons in Fischer-Random. Just like Kasparov he very often got the upper hand straight from the opening and drove home his advantage not in the last place thanks to his excellent technique and powerful concentration.

Later we discussed another form of Fischer-Random: any starting position without the mirror image. Once we had played a few moves in his flat we agreed that some starting positions were so bad for one side or the other that they could be considered lost.

On my way out after our Fischer-Random 'match' I walked past Bobby's collection of 11 or 12 pairs of Birkenstock clogs. A couple of weeks earlier Bobby had been furious when a photograph of his Birkenstock clogs had appeared in *Morgunbladid*. He blamed this breach of his privacy solely on Gardar. Bobby had told Gardar that a few of his clogs needed repair. They went to a shoemaker Gardar knew near the city centre. A few days later, knowing nothing of this, I told Bobby that I had seen pictures of what were called Bobby's clogs in an article about this shoemaker's shop in *Morgunbladid*. Bobby's rage was aimed at Gardar, who I believe had nothing to do with the article. Many months later, when *Morgunbladid* had an interview with Bobby about his fight with the Swiss UBS bank, he demanded and got an apology from editor Olafur Stephensson.

No matter what the weather was outside, he would always wear the Birkenstocks. Bobby held anything made in Germany in high regard. I was reminded of this preference when Saemi and I went to visit him at noon on December 24, 2005. I gave him a Christmas present, *The Da Vinci Code* by Dan Brown, with the inscription: 'Dear Bobby. It has been an eventful year. Merry Christmas, Helgi, Sigurborg, Olafur and Arnar Leo.'

On this occasion Bobby opened a bottle of red wine which Einar had given him and then he picked up a harmonica and played a tune for us. As he pointed out, from a large selection of harmonicas in the music store he had decided to buy a German one. I dared to bring up the subject of Bob Dylan's music and his skill with the harmonica, but Bobby was not very impressed. 'His music is all right,' he said, only to add in a bit of a killjoy spirit, 'but at the end of the day he is a Jew.'

Bobby liked to have a glass of wine, but never more than two. According to Dr. Kari Stefansson, an Icelandic neurologist and CEO and co-founder of deCODE Genetics, his moderate drinking could be connected with his being brought up in a Jewish environment where excessive drinking is seen as a serious flaw. If you drink too much you may lose control and Bobby never wanted to lose control. One day Bobby said to me: 'I have heard that chess players are drinking quite a bit nowadays. The only chess player who drank in the old days was Donner.' He went on to explain that his occasional urge to have a drink or two had something to do with what he called existential angst. He thought it was a good thing that the gods created spirits to soothe the pain of living.

Bobby could be amused by strange things. On the radio he liked to listen to AA meetings. He thought it weird that these people spoke so openly about their problems.

On another occasion he suddenly said: 'You know, Helgi, I almost became a smoker. I was sixteen or seventeen and I tried a cigarette. It was probably Camel or Viceroy. Then I had another cigarette. After a while I bought a pack of cigarettes. The I asked myself: Hey man, what are you doing? I just bought cigarettes! Cigarettes were not considered to be very harmful in those years, but it dawned on me that that I was on the wrong track. I threw away the cigarette pack. I never smoked after that.'

Chapter Eleven

He said, 'Wither away, Skarphedinn?'
'We shall fish for salmon, father.'
Njal's Saga

All sorts of people wanted to meet Bobby Fischer in the first days and weeks after his arrival in Iceland, and Bobby would talk freely to almost anyone. Viggo Hilmarsson was a senior manager at Straumur, an Icelandic investment bank. Bobby would later call him a 'bankster', but that was all right with Viggo. He was the only son of Hilmar Viggoson, who had been a member of the Icelandic Chess Federation during the 1972 match.

Viggo's father may well have told his son a few bedtime stories about the Great Match. I met him outside my home in early May 2005. We had met on another occasion at least once and I knew he was a keen follower of chess and a strong amateur player. Viggo asked for my assistance. A Canadian friend of his very much wanted Bobby to autograph a copy of My 60 Memorable Games. When I spoke with Bobby he was readily willing to sign the book. But he refused to sign the Faber & Faber copy I had brought him.

'It has to be a Simon and Schuster', he said. I didn't feel like asking him for the reason, but I knew the original publisher had been Simon & Schuster. The publication rights had been sold to Faber & Faber and the latest twist was when Batsford bought the rights from Faber & Faber and published an edition with the games in algebraic notation in 1995. According to the chess historian Edward Winter, British grandmaster John Nunn, who prepared the text for Batsford, made some 560 textual changes to the book. Fischer was furious about the Batsford edition and called the Batsford team 'criminals' and 'conspirators' at a press conference in Buenos Aires in 1996.

Probably the most painful change in the Batsford edition was a 'corrected' variation in Bobby's game against Bolbochan from the Stockholm interzonal of 1962. In the 'improved' line a check was overlooked that made the entire variation nonsensical. In any case I brought a copy of the Simon & Schuster hardback to Bobby's suite at the Hotel Loftleidir. Before he signed the book he asked: 'Is he a good person, this man?' 'Oh yes, I think so', I answered. Inside the book there was a one thousand krona bill, worth about 12 euros. Bobby smiled and put it in his wallet. Then he slowly signed the book.

Viggo was living with his wife above café Mokka in 101 Reykjavik. I knew the flat did not suit Bobby, but Viggo contacted me and said that he was willing to rent it to Bobby for a modest price as he and his wife had plans to build a house on the outskirts of Reykjavik. I went there with Bobby to take a look and he and Viggo got along fine. Viggo and his wife later invited Bobby to dinner and Viggo suggested that one day they could go fishing. In the end Bobby did not rent Viggo's apartment.

One day Viggo called me and proposed a fishing trip with Bobby. I knew he had gone fishing in a salmon river called Laxa in Kjos after the match in 1972. Bobby accepted the invitation and agreed to come with us. The trip took place at the end of August 2005.

The salmon river Gljufura runs through the northwestern part of Iceland. The best part of summer in Iceland for salmon fishing is usually July, but in this area you can expect to be quite successful in August or even the early part of September.

Viggo had initially intended to invite just me and Bobby, but I insisted that a friend of mine, an actor by the name of Johann Sigurdarson, should also come along. This turned out to be a good idea. We decided that Johann and I would pick Bobby up from his flat in Klapparstigur. Bobby let us in and Miyoko was there. She had arrived from Japan the night before. Apparently Bobby had not told her about the fishing trip.

Miyoko was living in Japan, but would come to Iceland every two or three months and stay there for at least 10 days. She had met Bobby the year after he became World Champion during his Asia trip in the fall of 1973. At the time she was studying pharmacy and later she graduated as a master of science. Afterwards she became the president of the Japanese Chess Federation and was working there full time as a general secretary when Bobby got in touch with her whilst living in Budapest.

'But I came yesterday', Miyoko said smilingly. 'This was planned months ahead', Bobby insisted, slightly apologetically. It was probably the only time I sensed some guilt on Bobby's part. I wondered whether we should also invite Miyoko, but the small size of the self-catering lodge that came with the fishing permit could have been a real obstacle. Besides, Viggo wasn't there, so I did not mention this possibility. Bobby kept on mumbling something, no hug or kisses, but then finally he waved Miyoko goodbye.

We made a stop at a shopping mall. As I went into a store for supplies, Bobby sat in the café on the first floor with Johann. Soon Bobby would start calling him Big Joe. When I came back half an hour later they were deep in conversation. Joe told me that while I had been shopping Bobby had received a phone call from his Icelandic lawyer, and now there was a serious change of mood. As we drove away I heard for the first time about Bobby's correspondence with the Swiss bank UBS, where he kept his earnings from the 1992 match. Bobby told us that shortly after his arrival in Iceland he had received a letter from UBS in which all business relations between the parties involved were terminated. As a result all his assets would be liquidated and sent to Landsbankinn, the national bank of Iceland. Bobby's lawyer had allowed UBS to make this transfer and this had enraged Bobby. We had to do some more shopping and I rather casually suggested that this turn of events had also been caused by pressure from abroad, most probably from the U.S. Justice Department.

'Of course. Goes without saying!' Bobby shouted back. He was becoming very irritated. Joe tried to explain to him that we were just trying to gather information. I 'blundered' horribly about his Icelandic lawyer when I asked: 'Is he on a commission or something?' This enraged Bobby even further, but I tried to keep calm since I knew that sometimes lawyers get a percentage of the amount at stake. We drove on and for the next 200 kilometres or so Bobby would not talk about anything but the UBS bank and we took a few 'punches' on behalf of the gigantic Swiss bank. At one point he called Landsbankinn and talked with a senior official from the bank. She confirmed that the bank had received a notice from UBS and a few million Swiss francs had been transferred to an account in his name in Landsbankinn. Bobby was furious: 'Send it back', he told the woman.

Our first stop was at a roadhouse café near a village built around the university at Bifrost. There we had a cup of coffee, Bobby ordered tea and kept on talking about the UBS bank. Our next stop was at a roadhouse café close to a bridge over Hrutarfjardar river, one of the more expensive salmon rivers in Iceland. Outside we spotted a leatherclad biker who looked familiar. 'Didn't we once play badminton with this guy?' I asked Joe. His name was Otto Jonsson and he was riding a Harley Davidson Road King from Reykjavik, heading north.

When he noticed that Joe was waving at him he walked to the car, had a few words with me and Joe but soon turned his attention to our sullen passenger in the front seat. It transpired that Otto had studied medicine in New York. 'So you were in the jungle', Bobby said, warming by the minute to the new acquaintance. 'Right. I was in the jungle.' Bobby laughed, and they had a pleasant conversation. Bobby could start a conversation with almost anyone. For us the important thing was that from then on the UBS matter was dropped. Not a word about it for the rest of the fishing trip.

We arrived late at the fishing hut and early the next morning we went fishing. We put a fishing rod into Bobby's hands. He was already in his boots and was armed with a tackle box, sunglasses, cap, gloves and sunscreen. The salmon rivers in Iceland are broken into sections, or beats, and each section has a story of its own, as is documented in the many river guides. Viggo went with Bobby to a spot very close to the fishing hut. Joe drove alone in his jeep. I stayed away, close to the fishing hut, practicing my golf swing. I had lost all interest in fishing long ago.

In less than five minutes Bobby's fishing rod all of a sudden began swinging and pumping furiously. Bobby's hands were trembling. 'Viggo, what the hell shall I do?' he shouted. 'Raise the fishing rod immediately!' Viggo shouted back.

Bobby had stumbled upon a remarkably stubborn salmon, but with Viggo's help they managed to land it in 15 minutes. When I walked over from the hut to where they were fishing it was Viggo's turn to try, but Bobby was pacing on the banks of the river watching Viggo's every move.

'So, what have you been up to?' I asked. 'I caught this one', Bobby answered, and pointed at the six-pounder. He was very quiet and looked like an ordinary fisherman on the banks of a river who had teamed up with an old friend.

At noon there was the customary break. We went into the fishing hut, where Bobby's catch was celebrated with a shot of whiskey. After the break I asked Bobby if he was going to try again. 'No,' he said, 'I am very happy with just one salmon. It's enough for me.' Big Joe and Viggo tried harder and were quite successful. When they came in at eight o'clock in the evening I prepared dinner for us, which was my own version of Spaghetti Bolognese with parmesan cheese, bread and a salad and some red wine. This was followed by a dessert.

At one point during dinner Bobby looked at me and said: 'This is good', something I had to take as a compliment. Big Joe had brought his guitar with him and a book of notes and lyrics. Soon after dinner he and Bobby started to jam. Bobby knew all the lyrics. We wondered how he had learned them so well. 'I was just listening to the radio', he said. 'But you must have had some records', I insisted. 'I think I once bought a record', Bobby said.

Big Joe has a well-trained voice. He has had leading roles in the National Theatre in musicals like Les Misérables, Fiddler on the Roof and The Sound of Music.

He has also sang in the opera a few times, and has been a member of a few bands. So Bobby was jamming with a pro. Still, he almost shouted when he thought Joe was singing out of tune.

'No, no, no. This is corny', he said, and proceeded to demonstrate how the song should be sung. He was very impressed by Big Joe. 'Do you know who my favourite radio host was? Big Joe Junior. He would come on late at night and this was his favourite sentence: "For anyone. You may be alone out there, but we are happy together."'

I envisioned the young Bobby Fischer alone in his Brooklyn flat listening to this disk jockey. Joe Rosenfield was the host of a radio talk show called 'The Happiness Exchange' for many years. He was also known as Big Joe, and his night-time show was called 'The Insomnia Stretch'. It was broadcast on several New York radio stations.

On many occasions 'our' Big Joe has been asked for a few Frank Sinatra standards. This evening he started out with New York, New York and then it was My Way. 'Regrets, I had a few...' 'Hey, this song is about Bobby', Viggo said. We got the point. Bobby was quiet for a while. He was bowing his head.

'C'mon Bobby. Don't be shy', I teased him a bit. When we made way for the old Tom Jones standard Green, Green Grass of Home it turned out we had totally misunderstood the lyrics. 'You see, the guy is waiting for his execution in a cell and the old padre is paying him the final visit before he is to be taken before the firing squad', Bobby explained to us.

At this point I opened the door and I noticed that it was a clear sky with millions of stars visible, and the northern lights were in full bloom. I called Bobby: 'Bobby. Have you ever seen the northern lights?' I asked him. He went out and gazed at the stars and this phenomenon that sometimes looks like curtains glowing above. He stood there for a very long time.

Shortly afterwards we took a walk outside the fishing hut. It was not much of an effort, but he was breathing heavily and I wondered about the status of his health. Then we returned. Bobby and Big Joe sang a few more standards and then Joe went to bed. But Bobby kept singing alone for a while. It was pitch dark, we had extinguished all the lights, but he kept pacing the floor of the fishing hut singing to himself. He was not a bad singer, but as I was lying in my bed I thought, when is this guy going to stop singing?

When I opened my eyes in the morning Bobby was already up. He was walking around the fishing hut talking to himself: 'The fucking Jews, they are after me, I must get to them. The fucking Jews.' And on and on. It was disturbing. Did he wake up every morning, day after day, week after week, year after year talking to himself like this?

I knew Bobby liked conspiracy theories, so I had brought a book with me about the JFK assassination, *Case Closed* by Gerald Posner, which I 'accidentally' left on my bed. He now turned his attention to the book and started to read. I told Bobby that I agreed with Posner's theories that Lee Harvey Oswald had acted alone.

'By the way, Bobby. Where were you when you heard about the assassination?' I asked. 'I was in my apartment in Brooklyn', Bobby replied. 'Let me see. Gerald Posner. The name suggests that he is from Poland. So I think there is a good chance he is a Jew.' After a while Bobby got tired of the book, but stated that it was highly unlikely that the theories put forward in it could hold water.

At about 12 o'clock we started to prepare for our departure. The rule was to leave the fishing hut in exactly the same condition as when we had arrived. Some work had to be done, washing the dishes and mopping the floor. Bobby participated in full. Everything was in order when we left the hut. Joe asked Bobby to sign for the fish he had caught in a special notebook. 'This is the custom in the salmon rivers of Iceland', he said. 'Nah, I don't think so', Bobby answered. 'Come on, Bobby you have to do it. Do it for us', I said. And Bobby Fischer signed for the salmon, a six-pounder. In the fishing record book he wrote: 'R. Fischer. Catch: salmon. Weight: 6 pounds.' Little could he know at that point that the proprietors of the river decided several years after his death to name the spot where he caught the fish after him.

When we came back to Reykjavik Miyoko was waiting for us. Bobby had phoned her on his mobile several times during the trip. We brought with us a big box with Bobby's catch. He opened it and proudly offered the fish to Miyoko. Like any other Japanese woman Miyoko knew how to handle a fish. She wet her hands and then stored it in the refrigerator. Afterwards she washed her hands with lukewarm soapy water.

'We must go fishing again soon', Big Joe said to Bobby. 'Yes, of course. Let's go again next week', he replied excitedly. I was very relieved. He had enjoyed the trip.

Chapter Twelve

But even when Njal was come into his bed, he heard that an axe came against the panel and rang loudly, but there was another shut bed, and there the shields were hung up, and he sees that they are away. He said, 'Who have taken down our shields?' 'Thy sons went out with them', says Bergthora.

Njal's Saga

In an interview with the German magazine *Der Spiegel*, published shortly before he played his World Championship match with Vladimir Kramnik in Bonn in the autumn of 2008, World Champion Viswanathan Anand mentioned his first and only meeting with Bobby Fischer: 'I played in a tournament in Reykjavik and the Icelandic grandmaster Helgi Olafsson asked me if I would be interested in meeting Bobby Fischer. Olafsson picked him up from his flat, while I waited in the car. Fischer probably wanted to avoid my knowing which apartment was his.'

Their meeting took place during the Glitnir blitz tournament in 2006 where Anand and Judit Polgar were special invitees. The event was staged in Reykjavik City Hall right after the traditional Reykjavik Open. The Reykjavik Open took place on the premises of the Reykjavik Chess Club and it was there that I saw Anand for the first time during this visit. One of the later rounds of the tournament was in progress. Magnus Carlsen was playing in Reykjavik for the second time, he had also played in 2004, and I was very impressed by him. He was no longer a kid but had matured into a great fighter.

Anand turning up at the open tournament took many players by surprise. When he saw me, he came up to me and we had a pleasant chat. I knew from Lilja Gretarsdottir, the president of the Icelandic Chess Federation, who had gone to meet him at the airport, that he would very much appreciate it if a meeting with Bobby could be arranged. I could see that he was pleased when I said: 'So, do you want to meet Bobby Fischer?'

To some people Bobby Fischer was some sort of an Elephant Man, a phenomenon they wanted to see or meet for the record and I was not especially helpful in those cases. In Anand's case things were different, of course. I am sure that like all serious chess players Anand had studied his games very carefully. After the round I called Bobby and told him that Anand wanted to meet him. Immediately he brought up an interview in *New In Chess* with

Anand about his match against Ivanchuk in Linares in 1993, where he had made some negative comments about the quality of the Fischer-Spassky match in Sveti Stefan and Belgrade. Trying to soften him up, I told Bobby that I had found his match in Sveti Stefan and Belgrade much more interesting and entertaining than the Anand-Ivanchuk match and that it was pointless to let some old comments prevent their meeting. At first he didn't give in, but then I recalled how positively Anand had spoken about *My 60 Memorable Games* and mentioned Anand's tough stance towards Kasparov. Gradually he 'surrendered' and agreed to meet him. Of course, he had his conditions: I would pick him up and they would go to a restaurant of his choice.

On the evening of Wednesday, March 17, I went to Hotel Baron, where Anand was staying, and together with his wife Aruna we drove to Bobby's apartment building. I parked my car in the small parking lot behind the building and we got out. As planned I phoned Bobby and told him we were there, and he said he would be with us in a few minutes. Seconds later my phone rang: 'Who is that with you?' an angry Bobby asked. 'It's Aruna, Anand's wife', I said.

'You promised me there would only be the three of us', Bobby retorted. 'Bobby, they are always together', I said. Instinctively it was the right thing to say, as Bobby seemed to get the impression that because of some Indian custom the wife would have to be present at important meetings. 'Why are you standing there? The fucking *DV* might be on your trail', Bobby blurted out. *DV* was a notorious tabloid paper.

Anand and Aruna were flabbergasted and Aruna asked me, 'Is it a problem that I am here?' 'No, no, don't worry. He is always like this. Let's get into the car and wait for him', I said. We sat in the car waiting and after a while Bobby appeared, walking briskly towards the car. I wondered what Anand was thinking, but I was sure it was an important moment for him.

Bobby sat down in the front seat. 'Hi', Bobby said shyly as he shook hands with Anand and Aruna. 'Can I call you Vishy?' he asked Anand. 'Yes, sure', Anand replied. Now Bobby turned to me. 'Let's see, where shall we go?' 'What about that Italian restaurant?' I asked. 'No, no, let's drive around a little. I am sure the fucking *DV* will be there.'

We drove around Reykjavik a bit and Bobby kept asking for directions to a fast-food restaurant he had been to. 'You should know about those places', he said to me. 'Well, actually I don't live in Reykjavik, but I am sure we will find that kind of place', I said, smiling.

He then turned to the passengers in the back seat: 'So, Vishy, what's going on in the chess world?' he asked. Anand told him he was playing more or less in the same tournaments in places like Wijk aan Zee, Linares, Monaco and Dortmund every year. 'Must be boring', Bobby said. 'No, I like it', Anand replied. 'So what are they playing now?' Bobby asked. Anand told him the English Attack in the Sicilian was all the rage and he mentioned that a very interesting variation in the King's Indian was much played. He also told Bobby that he was working a lot with the support of computer analysis.

I was still looking for the fast-food restaurant without much success when Bobby suggested that I should call my wife for directions. I stopped at a petrol station and Bobby strictly forbade me to use my mobile phone, insisting that I make a regular phone call inside the petrol station. Once inside I took out my mobile phone and called my wife who told me about a fast-food restaurant in Bolholt. In an interview with *The Times of India* Anand took it a bit further: 'He wouldn't let Helgi call his wife over the cell phone as he feared it might be tapped. Helgi had to cross over to the gas station and on the pretext of using the house phone, called his wife on the mobile for restaurant directions. We kept driving around remote parts of Reykjavik in Olafsson's car as we talked. Maybe it was his way of throwing the CIA off his trail.'

I had never been at the restaurant at Bolholt with Bobby before and I somehow felt his choice was a little out of character. He had mainly been frequenting restaurants in 101 Reykjavik, especially Thai restaurants, and seemed to hate fast food.

In the interview in *Der Spiegel* Anand said: 'Fischer told me how he sometimes rode around Reykjavik on the bus, in order to see the city. He complained that he could not get the Indian balm Amrutanjan in Iceland. Suddenly he wanted to go to McDonald's. So there he was, this legend of the chess world, asking me if I took ketchup.'

This account is not altogether correct. We certainly went to a fast-food restaurant, but Bobby would never have gone to a McDonald's. 'American-style' was fine, but he hated some big American companies, mainly because of their involvement in environmental controversies. Once we went to see a movie and when we arrived at the cinema I noticed that I had left my wallet in the car. As I went to get it I told Bobby to buy some popcorn. He joined the queue and when I got back he handed me the popcorn. 'You forgot the coke', I said, 'I also want a coke.' And he replied, 'That you'll have to get yourself', and he handed me a 500 Kroner bill. We both had a good laugh. He would never buy Coca Cola.

When we were about to order Anand politely mentioned that he and his wife were vegetarians. But he nevertheless had fish and chips and when we sat down Bobby pulled out his worn pocket chess set. Anand tried to show him a chess problem but I knew the only item on the agenda would be some 'prearranged' games between Karpov and Kasparov in their 1984/85 match.

On several occasions Bobby claimed that not only had all the Kasparov versus Karpov matches been prearranged move by move, but also most of the old World Championship matches. He always stressed that if he could point out one example of clear misconduct it would prove his theory. Actually the example he put forward this evening was intriguing and for a moment it seemed he had a point. As he described it later, Anand felt a generation gap when Bobby pulled out a pocket chess set to show him the position. The chess set was of German origin, in fine leather. Bobby put up a position from the 36th game of the first match between Kasparov and Karpov. After 14 moves a position was reached that had also occurred in the first game of the World Championship match between Kortchnoi and Karpov in Baguio in 1978. In that game Kortchnoi played a quiet move and three moves on the game ended in a draw.

However, in the game that Kasparov and Karpov played on December 28, 1984, White continued with the most logical move in the position, 15.♘e5, a move that both sides should have seen if they had prepared this opening. The move looks natural, but as Bobby pointed out, only two moves further on Karpov could have played a move (17...♛b8 instead of 17...♝a6 as he played) which according to Bobby would have given Black 'a winning position'. His question, and to his mind further proof of the fact that the match was prearranged, was why White took such a risk with his 15th move while he was 1-5 down and Karpov only needed one more win to clinch the match?

Unfortunately for Bobby, things were not that clear. His 'winning move' wasn't that winning and as he and Anand analysed he could not prove his point. In some instances Black was even losing.

After we left the restaurant we drove towards Anand's hotel. It was not very far away from Bobby's building. When Anand and Aruna were about to get out of the car, Bobby rose from his seat. 'I must follow you out', he said. I witnessed another example of the shy, courteous and likeable Bobby Fischer. They exchanged some pleasant words and I really felt they liked each other.

Viggo Hilmarsson shows his skills at fly fishing.

'Big Joe', actor Johann Sigurdarson, in Arthur Miller's *All My Sons* at the Icelandic National Theatre.

Free at last. Bobby Fischer in good spirits, with Miyoko Watai at his side.

Bobby making a point during the welcome dinner in Hotel Holt. My wife Sigurborg and I listen to what he has to say.

For two years Bobby lived on the fourth floor at Klapparstigur 5.

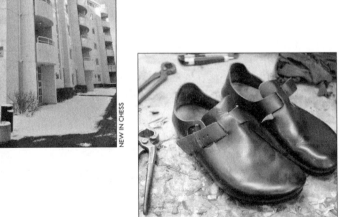

Bobby's Birkenstock clogs.

During a trip to Nesjavellir, close to Thingvellir, Bobby was very excited about the geothermal power station.

January 1, 2007. 'Do it for us, Bobby.' (L. to R.) Asta Karen Rafnsson, Thorsteinn Thorgeirsson, Miyoko Watai, Bobby Fischer, Kantathi Suphamong and I.

Bobby with Thorsteinn and Kantathi Suphamong. This is probably the last photo that was taken of him.

At Bobby's tombstone in Laugdælakirkja.

Anand asked Bobby if he could have a photograph of him. 'It will just be for my private use. I'll put the photo on the desktop of my laptop', Anand said. He did not get Bobby's approval, but it was fine with Anand.

'Yes. I think Anand got a better upbringing than I did', Bobby said as we drove away. I did not say anything. His words struck me as a sudden revelation of a difficult childhood. The meeting stayed with Anand and he has mentioned it on several occasions. Returning triumphantly from his victory over Vladimir Kramnik to India as World Champion in the autumn of 2008 he paid tribute to Bobby. The Times of India quoted him as saying: 'I mean, most of modern chess is his offering. Myself and the rest had those moves ready for us when we started out, but it had to take someone to discover them first. Bobby Fischer was that person. He was that person for entire generations of chess players. His was a singular life in that sense. He's made it easier for us today.'

Chapter Thirteen

Now these tidings come to the Thing, and Njal made them tell him the tale thrice, and then he said — 'More men now become man-slayers than I weened.'
Njal's Saga

On August 15, 2006, I celebrated my 50th birthday. I had no plans for anything special, since at that time of year a lot of people are on holiday. After a round of golf I had a small reception with sandwiches and beer at the golf club. Earlier that day I had called Bobby and asked him whether he would join me and my wife Sigurborg for dinner at Sjavarkjallarinn, a restaurant in the centre of Reykjavik. Big Joe was also going to come. Bobby accepted the invitation and in the early evening we drove over to pick Bobby up from his flat at Klapparstigur.

'How old do you think I am?' I asked. 'Well, I don't know. 42?' he replied. 'No, I am 50', I said. 'Oh, you look great.' We got to the place a few minutes later and in a darkened room at the restaurant I raised a glass and said a few words: 'To Bobby and Joe. To two very special guys. Thank you for coming.' After we had ordered I turned to Bobby and asked him very directly, 'All right, Bobby. What was your secret?' He looked at me with a slightly surprised expression. 'Someone put it exactly right. The secret of Bobby Fischer is that there is no secret', he answered. It almost sounded as if he was not talking about himself. 'Come on', I said. 'You must have had something?'

'I think I had good concentration. I also sat well', he said. He did not mention his uncompromising attitude towards the game itself, nor his greatest pleasure, 'to break a man's ego', as he had famously described it in the television interview with Dick Cavett in 1971. To my mind there had been a forceful combination of character traits and external circumstances that had driven him. Compared to him, some of his Soviet colleagues almost looked like wimps.

As we were eating he turned the conversation to an all-too-familiar subject, his hatred of 'the Jews'. 'Don't you ever get tired of fighting the Jews?' Sigurborg asked Bobby. 'Well, someone has to do it', he said. The answer offered me an opportunity I jumped at. 'But Bobby, are you not on thin ice? After all, your mother is Jewish', I said. I didn't expect him to be happy about my question, but I shrank back from asking him about his real father, Paul Nemenyi, who after all was Jewish too. 'Look. What happened somewhere more than 60 years ago does not matter at all', he said. 'Anybody can become a Jew. It is a religious matter.'

Later that evening Sigurborg went home, but the three of us walked to a wine bar close to the parliament square. As we entered, a man I knew exclaimed in Icelandic: 'So it is your turn now for the shift!' – meaning that Bobby had to be such an intolerable person that the small group around him had to socialize with him every now and then in turns. I decided not to answer him, but I did not exclude the possibility that by the tone of the man's voice Bobby understood the meaning of his words, even though he spoke no Icelandic. He asked me: 'What did he say?' 'Oh, it was nothing. Just another bitter vampire', I answered. A new round of drinks was brought to our table, but as usual Bobby's intake of wine was modest.

Big Joe turned the conversation to a possible comeback. 'Don't you want to play again?' he asked. 'Of course I want to play', Bobby answered. 'But you are in no shape', Big Joe said. 'For you it is the same as for some old actor who has been away from the scene for a long time. He has to get into shape. Or a boxer who has lost some of his former glory. When he starts to go downhill the only thing he is looking for is his old locker-room in the ghetto. You have to start working. The Icelandic grandmasters can go with you to some training camp and work with you. Then you will be ready. No sooner. No later.' Big Joe had become very excited about the prospect of Bobby working on a comeback.

'The old jaded Bobby Fischer', as he had once laughingly described himself, actually took Big Joe's words seriously. He sat almost motionless against the wall in his chair at the wine bar.

In the following months there would be moments when we would talk about possible plans for a match and he would invariably say: 'We have to talk to Big Joe about this.' On one such occasion he added, 'I think you are very lucky to have a friend like Big Joe.'

A few months later, in November, two friends of mine from the Westman Islands, Asmundur Fridriksson and Arni Sigfusson, organized a nine-round birthday tournament for me in Keflavik. The well-known international airport of Reykjavik takes its name from this town. All the best players in Iceland were invited. Asmundur and Arni very much wanted to have Bobby to come over and visit the tournament. I tried to persuade him and he almost agreed, but then he decided that too many people would be there, so he didn't come.

Christmas was approaching and I was shopping on December 9 when Lilja Grétarsdottir, the president of the Icelandic Chess Federation, called me and asked if I could be at the TV station in two hours as a commentator for the final match of the Icelandic Championship in rapid chess. Little did I suspect at that moment that that television appearance would produce my most famous chess column. The preparatory work for the program by RUV, the state-run TV company, had been sloppy. At one point the demonstration board even broke down and for a long time it was impossible to give any sensible explanation to the audience. In spite of these problems and the mistakes they made themselves in the middlegame, the finalists, international masters Arnar Gunnarsson and Bragi Thorfinnsson, nevertheless managed to create some interesting positions and entertain the spectators.

As I was watching TV later in the evening at my home, the phone rang. Bobby Fischer was on the line. 'I saw you on the television today', he said rather quietly. 'You know, the guy could have played take on g2 and then played ♖h4.' I was astonished by the move he suggested and immediately understood what he meant. Still, even more than that I was happy, even elated, that he had immersed himself in chess and called me about what he had found. We spoke about the game and I was critical about several decisions the players had made. Bobby listened but kept silent about that.

A few days later I met Pétur Blöndal, a journalist from Morgunbladid, and told him about Bobby's phone call. 'Hey man, this is big news', he said. 'You must get Bobby's approval to write about it.'

I called Bobby and asked him for permission to write about his suggestion. 'Yes, it's OK', he said. 'But first come over and check the variations with me.' I went to Bobby's flat and we went through the variations. It was interesting to watch how very exact Bobby was when diligently going through every line. I went home and wrote the article, which was published on December 16, 2006. Here is the relevant part:

'The phone rang and Bobby Fischer was on the line. He told me he had seen the broadcast. The topic of our discussion was the final position of the game:

Bragi Thorfinnsson – Arnar Gunnarsson

In this position Arnar blundered by playing 37...♔g8 and naturally there came 38.♕xg7 mate. The explanation is simple, he was ahead of himself as he had intended to play 37...♕d7 first. In reaction to that move Fischer pointed out an ingenious combination: 37...♖xg2+ 38.♔h1 ♖h4!! – note that 38.♔xg2 does not work because of 38...♖g4+ and 39...♕g2 mate. After 38...♖h4 39.♕f7+ fails because of the discovered check 39...♖g7+, while 39.f3 is answered by 39...♖g1+ and mates as Fischer pointed out: 40.♔h2 ♕c2+ or 40.♖xg1 ♕xf3+ etc.

It was, of course, a privilege to discuss chess with Bobby Fischer. Innumerable books have been written about his chess-playing skills and some authors have tried to unlock the mystery of his play. In 1972 three thousand people stared at the enormous demonstration board in Laugardalshöll when the sixth game of the 'Match of Century' was being played, among them many very strong players. All sorts of moves were speculated about when Spassky played his 19th move. Then the simplest move on earth appeared on the demo board, 20.e3-e4. Not a single soul in the playing hall had thought of it, as Fridrik Olafsson explained in his book about the match.

When we were analysing together, it struck me that Bobby did not criticize either Bragi or Arnar. He was not boastful at all but pondered every move objectively, which in chess is a cardinal virtue.

A 'trained eye' can grasp certain patterns on the chessboard. During a tournament game strong players sometimes draw all sorts of analogies and think of comparable situations they have seen. Let me give an example:

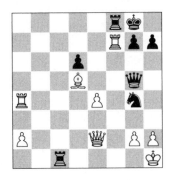

Bobby Fischer – James Sherwin
New York 1957

The feat of 14-year-old Bobby Fischer winning the U.S. Championship in 1957 was big news. In this position the young Fischer played: 31.♕f1!!

The theme of discovered check is reminiscent of the game between Arnar and Bragi. It turns out that Black is completely defenceless. Sherwin played 31...h5 but was taken by surprise again: 32.♕xc1! – Black loses a rook, as 32...♕xc1 is answered by 33.♖f1+.

This was one of the first articles I contributed to *Morgunbladid* and it was around this time that I began to write for the paper on a regular basis. Even if it was in Icelandic, Bobby was curious about the piece and asked me 'Where can I have it?' I had the feeling that he was pleased that the move he had found had appeared in print and he wanted to see it. I didn't think that he wanted to check if he agreed with what I had written, his curiosity was based on a positive sentiment. Still, when I started to write more I was not always sure he liked my connection to the press.

Chapter Fourteen

Then Gunnar said to Hallgerda, 'Give me two locks of thy hair, and ye two, my mother and thou, twist them together into a bowstring for me.' 'Does aught lie on it?' she says. 'My life lies on it', he said.

Njal's saga

While I was shopping in the huge Kringlan mall in the new centre of Reykjavik, about four kilometres from the old town, on December 31, 2006, a man came up to me who introduced himself as Thorsteinn Thorgeirsson. He told me that a friend of his, Kantathi Suphamong, was coming to Iceland to spend the holidays with him and his family. Kantathi Suphamong was the former foreign minister of Thailand. He had been living in exile since September 2006 when the military junta had overthrown the interim government of his close friend Thaksin Shinawatra.

Suphamong happened to be the president of Thailand's chess association and according to Thorsteinn he was eager to meet Bobby. Thorsteinn asked for my assistance in this matter, so I went over to Bobby. Miyoko answered the door and I said, 'I knew you were going to be here for the New Year.' This was just small talk, a way of greeting her, but much to my surprise Bobby reacted quite vehemently to my words and shot a question at me: 'How did you know this?' I didn't react as I didn't have anything sensible to say to his question, but I had noticed that of late he had become more and more suspicious about very innocent things.

Miyoko had arrived for a visit to Iceland the night before and I told them about the conversation I had had with Thorgeirsson. Bobby did not rule out the possibility of a meeting, but, as he put it, 'First we have to google this guy.' Together we did some research about the former Thai foreign minister, and after I had left Bobby continued his investigations. Around 4 in the afternoon he called me saying it was fine. But he added, 'I am going just with Miyoko.' I only had to drive them there. I felt slightly offended, because I thought his wish was connected to his sudden question about how I knew that Miyoko would be in Iceland, but as I had something else to do in the course of the evening anyway, I didn't say anything and gave Thorsteinn a call.

The next day, on January 1, at around 8 pm, I drove Bobby and Miyoko to Thorsteinn's home in Bryggjuhverfi, a part of Reykjavik down by the ocean. When we were inside, Bobby suddenly turned to me and, trying to be as friendly as possible, he whispered, 'You can join us.' But as I had another appointment, I only stayed for half an hour. Bobby and Miyoko spent a pleasant evening with Thorsteinn's family and Kantathi Suphamong and his wife. Before I left Thorsteinn wanted to take some photographs, but, as usual, Bobby refused. He gave in when, as in similar cases before, I said, 'Come on Bobby, do it for us.' These photos are probably the last ones taken of him.

One year later, after Bobby's death, Kantathi Suphamong wrote about the meeting in a touching article. It was published on January 27, 2008, in the Thai newspaper *The Nation* and was called 'A Song for Bobby Fischer'. The following fragment is taken from his article:

'...(Thorsteinn) told me that Fischer was in town and he would try to invite him to dinner. I agreed, even though it was well known that Fischer did not like to socialize. But Fischer accepted the invitation and arrived with his partner Miyoko Watai. He said he had come after googling my name and coming up with some interesting information. He wanted to meet me. He expressed his well-known views on the United States and the Jewish community. He then impressed me with his knowledge of Thailand and the political situation here, explaining that over the years he had spent much of his time listening to the BBC World Service.

'As far as chess was concerned, he said it was no longer a strategy game. Instead of coming up with original moves, players would only use strategies memorized from books. That was the reason he introduced what he called "Fischer-Random", which requires pieces to be placed on the board randomly at the beginning of the game, so players cannot revert to old strategies from memory.

'After I returned to Thailand, Bobby Fischer began to e-mail me. He had kind words for me, saying it had been "truly a great pleasure and honour" to meet me. He also said, "I'm glad to see that there are still some people in the heart of things who are full of good will!" He asked me about the "red rain phenomenon that fell over Kerala, India in 2001", saying that I should check it out via Google. In a later e-mail, he expressed concern about news reports that Israel may have been planning a nuclear strike on Iran's nuclear facilities. He mentioned that one of the reasons why he was "so unpopular" to certain people was because he had "a long memory".

'In one of the last e-mails to me, he discussed the new airport in Thailand. He then asked me whether I had a Siamese cat. He wrote that Siamese cats were very different from Western cats and that he remembered them from an old Walt Disney movie. He concluded that Siamese cats were "very aristocratic!" That was the side of Fischer that I got to know. It was a human side showing a man with a deep interest in world affairs and with a sense of humour.'

In his article Kantathi Suphamong skipped one important issue. That evening, while I was still there, Bobby also brought up the miserable condition of prisoners in Thailand who, according to some news reports Bobby had read, often suffocated to death. His remark met with total silence and caused a brief uncomfortable moment.

The following day, January 2, Bobby asked me to come over to his place. Miyoko was there and so was Gudmundur Thorarinsson, who had been invited as well. When I asked Bobby how the evening had been, he said 'Oh, it was OK.' It was clear he had other things on his mind and wanted to discuss them. He wanted to talk about a match. It was the start of a new year and he seemed desperate to make plans, to talk about projects. He was agitated and restless, and at some point he even suggested I fly to Japan for a reason I do not remember. When later that day Gudmundur and I left the building, we cast each other a meaningful look. Something was not going right.

The match Bobby wanted to talk about now was different from the one he had proposed last summer, a match with Britney Spears! He had read an article in a British tabloid that reported on Britney Spears' love life. After he had read this he told me in all seriousness: 'She and Justin Timberlake would be making love all day, only taking a break to play some chess... A match between me and Britney Spears would be a fine business idea. A sort of a Beauty and the Beast contest!' He knew a lot about business ideas and this one wouldn't be such a bad one, he thought. Still, I was never sure how serious his plans were, either concerning a match with Britney Spears or a match against one of the leading players of the day. Actually I was not too happy to be involved in any of those either, as I never knew if these projects were just to keep him busy or if he really wanted to play.

That evening he was impatient and irritated. He was becoming bored in Iceland and may have felt he was more and more a prisoner in our country. As a result of our discussions I sent Anand an email. He called me and we had a friendly conversation. I talked about Bobby's plans and he replied in a friendly and diplomatic manner. We both must have had the same feeling, that we were talking about something that was never going to happen, but we never expressed that thought. Perhaps I was hoping for a miracle to happen, as it made me sad to see Bobby waste his time.

To keep that hope alive I went to see Bobby to draw up a list of 18 points describing the details of a match against Anand. We couldn't decide on all issues, or rather Bobby couldn't, as I was mostly merely writing down what he was saying. To begin with it should obviously be a Fischer-Random match with draws not counting. Sometimes he would also call it Chess960, as the German organizer Hans-Walter Schmitt did, who staged several Chess960 tournaments in Mainz. Bobby actually liked this name for his invention.

The winner would be the first player to win 'x number of games'. I guess he had 10 wins in mind, but we didn't specify the number as he wanted to discuss it with his opponent. The speed of play he had in mind was 90 minutes for the entire game plus a 30-second increment per move. Faster time-controls were possible, but in that case the number of wins should be increased.

The prize-fund should be in 'tens of millions of dollars'. I knew there was little use discussing this and I simply wrote it down. Bobby had an interesting principle in these matters. He told me: 'You never get what you deserve. You only get what you negotiate.'

The match should be held either in Iceland or in a 'pollution-free location somewhere in India.' Bobby knew he could be arrested again if he left the country, but he expected the match organizers to guarantee his security. When on a different occasion we talked about a match in the Philippines, he suggested a military escort, so that the US government couldn't intervene.

Three or four games should be played a week and Bobby would own the videos after the match. That this was a slightly anachronistic demand I didn't tell him. It was obvious that he simply copied this idea from the 1972 match.

The match should be played according to 'standard rules' and his new but not yet released simplified chess clock should be used.

His ideas about the dates said a lot about his impatience during these discussions. The match should be played in the 'spring or summer of 2007'. For several reasons the sponsor or sponsors should be Indians. After all, India was an independent country and there were technical reasons as well. As he put it, 'They have computer wizards over there.' Both the Internet coverage and television should be arranged by Indians too. And, taking a leaf out of Mr. Titomirov's book, he suggested an Internet fee of 10 USD worldwide per game, or more for the whole match.

An unexpected and original idea for me was his suggestion to have the brand name of the sponsor right on the board, faded but visible. He could not make up his mind about the flag he was to play under. We left that issue undecided, but it was clear to me that he was not eager to play under the Icelandic flag. Obviously there should be a private room for the players backstage and, having mentioned that, he came to the final point which said that he was 'ready to play at any time during the day.' Why he included that, I don't know, but it almost looked as if he wanted to stress his flexibility in this matter.

I never wanted to make a cent off Bobby and almost always paid when we went somewhere together. When I contacted Anand I also stressed that obviously there was nothing in it for Iceland or me if the match came about. Still, even if I didn't believe any such match would ever take place, I suddenly couldn't suppress bringing up my role after I had written down his list of points. I turned to Bobby and said, 'If I am going to be involved in this, maybe we should make a deal. You will have to pay me.' I don't remember his exact words, but he didn't need to think this over. Immediately he told me he could not do that and that I would get nothing. Full stop.

After I had sent Bobby's list to Anand, his reply came quickly:

Dear Helgi,
Sorry for not replying earlier. Please give me some time to get back on this. I am busy till April with tournaments so I have asked my people in India to look at the possibilities of this event. Please convey my wishes personally to Bobby and I still remember with great warmth our last meeting.
Regards and all the best in 2007.
Vishy

In the meantime I kept asking myself why this attempt to organize another Fischer match should succeed. His ideas about the prize money were simply out of proportion to begin with. Apparently I was not the only one to have doubts. On May 9, 2007, Anand replied in another e-mail:

Dear Helgi,
Unfortunately I have been busy with tournaments. Although it will be an honour to play Bobby I am not able to guarantee the conditions he has asked

for. Maybe after Mexico in September we can speak about it again. Sorry for not replying as I was in a training camp which just finished today.
Regards
Anand

It was clear to me that with his busy schedule, Anand simply would not allow himself to engage in any further talks about a match and thus invest time and energy in protracted negotiations. When I forwarded the e-mail to Bobby he got the message. He sensed that Anand was not interested and was deeply wounded. He said we had to be active on more than one front and talk about other matches too. 'If we have more than one thing going that will keep the people guessing.' He asked me to contact Kasparov's 'head-quarters', and I called his manager, Owen Williams, twice. He explained to me that Garry's political plans were such that all serious chess matters other than his writings had been laid to rest. That was essentially the end of our plans for a match with Anand or Kasparov. As I see it now, the best and strongest move would have been simply to call a press conference and issue a Bobby Fischer challenge to either Kasparov or Anand.

It became clear to me around this time that Bobby's health was deteriorating fast. He didn't look well. The man that appears in the rare last pictures no longer looks like the strong, sturdy man that arrived in Iceland. Still, he managed to conceal his problems when we met in the first months in 2007, probably because of the drive and energy with which he tried to look for a new 'project'. We never talked about his health. Not because I didn't want to help him, but he simply didn't allow you to bring it up.

Occasionally we would still go to the cinema. We had also planned to make a trip together with Gudmundur Thorarinsson, with whom he was now in contact more than before. Bobby wanted to go to Stykkisholmur, in the western part of Iceland. He was even talking about renting a house there. He would sometimes complain about his life in Reykjavik, 'I have to get out of this place'. He was bored and wanted to be somewhere else, 'as far away from the aluminium plants as possible!' Those plants were in the Reykjavik area and were among the environmental issues that constantly worried him. He would complain about the chlorine in the swimming pools in Reykjavik or about the airport close to the old centre.

Naturally he was also opposed to the Karanjukar Dam that was being built in the eastern part of Iceland. I told him that there was a political party waiting for him, the Left Green Party. He didn't say anything. Still he must have had thoughts about a political role he could play. He once stunned me by asking out of the blue: 'Is it possible to rule Iceland from abroad?' He didn't say why he asked and I was too perplexed to answer, but there was no doubt that he was talking about himself. He didn't say either from where he would want to rule Iceland if it were possible. Perhaps he was thinking about Hong Kong, where he had been many times. More than once he told me: 'The best meals I ever had were in Hong Kong.'

He knew there was a risk he'd be arrested if he left the country and never talked about going somewhere. Except for once, in 2006, when there were charter flights from Iceland to Cuba around Christmas. We were having a drink with Big Joe and I suggested going there on a holiday and he said that wasn't a bad idea. But of course nothing happened.

At the beginning of April I invited him to a concert at NASA, at the time the most popular night club in Reykjavik. Afterwards we dined at Italia, one of his favourite restaurants. It was the last time I saw him.

My last conversation with Bobby took place on the evening of Saturday May 5, 2007. He made the phone call and we talked for two hours. He told me he had been approached by some people in the streets of Reykjavik who asked him to pose for a photograph with him, 'and I said no.' He was very upset and very distraught about the documentary film *Me and Bobby Fischer*. He felt betrayed by Saemi and voiced his opinions in a very grim way. Bobby told me that it was true that he had agreed to take part in a documentary film about the 'kidnapping in Japan', as he put it, but as it turned out the makers of the film, Fridrik Gudmundsson and Kristinn Hrafnsson, and Saemi had something totally different in mind. They wanted to make a film about Saemi's friendship with Bobby, which they had never mentioned to him before, and that's what the film turned out to be about.

I had heard from Saemi's brother Magnus that Saemi had received some very unpleasant text messages from Bobby. He went totally overboard and they were so weird that Saemi didn't even want to talk about them. Fridrik Gudmundsson, the producer of the documentary, had called and asked for my assistance in bringing Bobby back to the project. I had been unwilling to cooperate, as I knew from the start that it was a doomed project.

Bobby and I had talked till 2 am. Around 7.30 in the morning my mobile phone woke me up with a text message from Bobby. He was probably still awake and he wanted to spoil my day. His message put an end to our friendship, for a while at least. It started off rather innocently saying that in the last two years we had had many long conversations and then he went into a rage, angry that I hadn't manage to arrange the matches with Anand and Kasparov and furious that my stance against Saemi had not been tough enough. The most memorable line was: '... please pay me 10,000 USD sincere money so as to prove which side you are on.'

I know that I should have replied with a simple OK, and left it at that for the moment. Maybe that's what I wanted to do, but at the same time I strongly felt that this time I would have to wait for a long time for him to calm down. My reaction was too harsh and I regret it. I had always confronted Bobby and he valued that. I guess one should never write anything when angry and the e-mail I sent him was certainly not polite. What I wrote about Iceland was a reaction to him calling Iceland a 'fifth-class nation' in our nocturnal talk.

The New York whiners were inspired by a story about Mother Theresa, who had so many demands when she was once staying in a New York hospital that a journalist concluded that she had quickly become a New York whiner. This is what I wrote: '... About the 10,000 USD. Forget it. In general I think Americans are obsessed with money. And New Yorkers are whiners. That includes you. Icelanders may be inferior to Germans but we saved your ass – not the Germans or any other country. It is true however that nothing has come out of efforts to bring about a match between you and Kasparov or Anand. The thing is that both Kramnik and Topalov have expressed willingness to play you. You should perhaps hire a professional agent. I realize that you are very bitter about the documentary film and rightly so but I have nothing to do with this film...'

In reply to my email he sent me a final text message: 'Your groveling article in the *Reykjavik Grapevine* showed your true colours.'

The *Reykjavik Grapevine* is a free magazine that you can pick up at any petrol station in Iceland. The editor hails from New York. Shortly before Bobby came to Iceland they called me. I helped them with photographs and talked to their reporter. At one point in his story he quoted me as saying that in Iceland there was no Jewish problem. This was a quote out of context as obviously I didn't say anything racist, but simply referred to the fact that there are not many Jews in Iceland. Still, it sounded a bit clumsy and a reader wrote a letter taking me to task for this remark. I replied to his letter saying that if he had read the whole of the interview he would have seen that I was not an anti-Semite and that it has always been my philosophy to judge any individual by his or her merits.

Apparently Bobby had read this when he came to Iceland. He had never mentioned it before. Now he did.

But these things were not only happening to me. From other quarters I heard that Bobby was making impossible demands for a public condemnation of Saemi. And by this time he had also fallen out with Gudmundur. During a visit to his house Bobby had suddenly started to query Gudmundur about the gate money in 1972, wondering if everything had been done honestly. Taken aback, Gudmundur had said that he didn't know if the Federation still had the accounts but that he would try to find them and show them to Bobby. By then Bobby had already gotten so excited and angry that he told him, 'You're not talking like an innocent man. And don't talk to me again till you show me that contract.' The contract could not be found and Gudmundur let the matter rest, knowing that there was little he could do.

After this bitter exchange of text messages and emails there was no contact between Bobby and me. In the following months I expected to run into Bobby on the streets of Reykjavik one day. I spoke to Bragi Halldorsson, who had seen him in downtown Reykjavik. His conclusion was that Bobby definitely was in need of medical care.

In the autumn of 2007 I was travelling a lot. Then in October I heard that Bobby was in the hospital. I didn't know what exactly was the matter with him, but I had heard that he had kidney problems. I contacted Gardar, who of all the RJF people was seeing him most by then and whom I occasionally called. I asked him to give Bobby my regards. In early December Magnus Skulason told me that Bobby had been discharged from the hospital. Around this time a Reykjavik magazine wrote that Bobby Fischer had shrugged off all the gossip about a serious illness when he was spotted at the cinema in the Kringlan mall. He was there to see the film *American Gangster*, set in the late sixties and early seventies, with Denzel Washington and Russell Crowe. It was probably the last film he ever saw.

Chapter Fifteen

*At that point, on the verge of daybreak, there was a scream of sirens. They were
announcing a departure to a world towards which I would now be forever indifferent.*
Albert Camus, *The Outsider*

On January 16, 2008 I drove to Thorlakshöfn, a small village on the
south coast of Iceland. From its harbour a ferry sails to the Westman
Islands twice a day. The trip from Thorlakshöfn takes about three hours and
I have taken this route quite often over the past few years. The other option
is to fly from Reykjavik Airport, but the weather is very often unstable and
people sometimes wait for hours for the planes to take off.

Bobby had mentioned that during a trip with Gardar to the southern part
of Iceland he noticed the islands rising up from the sea. He wondered how
difficult it had been for me to travel from the Westman Islands to Reykjavik and asked me whether I had seen many of the games in the '72 match. I
told him that I had been in the playing hall for five of the games because that
summer, as was the custom for young people of my age in those days, I was
working in a fish factory. I explained to him that at the time it was considered
normal for children even 14 or 15 years old to work in the fish factories for
up to 16 hours a day, and that Westman Islanders play as hard as they work.

We had planned to go there in the summer of 2006. Bobby had stressed
the importance of going by boat. I think he would have liked the ferry trip. I
had contacted Arni Johnsen, a member of parliament and a sort of ambassador
for the Westman Islands, and he readily offered to show us around. But it was
difficult to find suitable dates and we decided to postpone the trip until the following summer, as it was clear that Bobby really wanted to go there. Unfortunately that trip didn't come about either, as a couple of months later we fell out.

When I arrived on Heimaey I gave chess lessons for the kids at the club
during the day and after a break we continued in the evening. The program
was the same the next day, but after dinner I gave a simul for everybody.
About thirty participated, mostly kids. I had forgotten to shut down my
mobile phone and all of a sudden it rang. Instead of answering I turned off
the mobile and proceeded with the simul. A young boy of about 10 years
old asked me: 'Should you not lose all the games since your phone rang?'
Everybody started to laugh and I said to him that according to the new rules
about mobile phones he was probably right.

A few minutes later the door of the clubhouse opened and a man in his early 70s entered almost dramatically. Everyone knew who he was, but he had never been to the chess club before and as he entered everyone turned around in some surprise. He looked at me and said aloud: 'You have surely grown up since the last time I saw you.' Then he walked out again, slammed the door and left. Some of the older participants smiled and so did I. When the simul was about to end my mobile rang again. I decided to answer and there was a journalist on the line. 'We have heard from a staff member at Landspitalinn [the national hospital] that Bobby Fischer died there today. Can you confirm this?' the voice asked. I asked him to call later.

I did not say a word to anyone and when the simul was over I left and drove around the island. I felt that the news was true and decided to call Fridrik Olafsson. He had heard about it too but there was no confirmation. We agreed that this could not be a false rumour.

'I am going to have a drink somewhere', I told Fridrik. I headed for a bar owned by an old friend of mine, Throstur Johnsen, Arni's brother. He was not in, but I ordered a glass of chilled white wine and sat alone in a corner for a long time. A glass is a glass. Now it dawned on me that I was actually sitting on the ground floor of Drifandi, 'the house of energy'. Here, on the first floor, I had visited a chess club for the first time more than forty years ago in 1968. Then I had been here with some of the younger players like Gudni Gunnarsson and Einar Otto Hognason, who had lent me the book How not to play chess. The smell of cigarettes, players writing down their moves, it all came back to me. I even met the police commissioner, Freymodur, a man with very thick eyebrows and a deep voice, who came there one Sunday in December at the start of the championship. And I remembered what Johannes had said before the Vasiukov simul in the spring of 1968, and that his mention of a certain Bobby Fischer had become a prophecy.

At 8.15 the next morning, January 18, the ferry sailed back to Thorlakshönd. I knew this was going to be a tough day. I wasn't able to reach Gardar by phone, but at about 10.30 I received a call from him. It was short and he confirmed that Bobby had died around noon on the 17th. About that time the news broke out all over the world. Journalist Sigtryggur Sigtryggsson phoned me from Morgunbladid and I decided to give him all the details about Bobby's attempt to play Anand. He asked me whether I had sent in my article for Saturday's paper. 'No', I said. 'We want you to write an obituary for Morgunbladid', he replied.

As I drove from Thorlakshöfn to Reykjavik I called a few friends informing them about Bobby's death. A short interview with me appeared on the website of *Morgunbladid*: 'My heart is filled with sorrow. An overpowering regret about the difficulties he endured during his life.'

Back at my home I started working on the obituary, but the phone rang constantly. I knew it would take some time to digest what had happened and it was good to be doing something. I gave an interview to two channels of the BBC. I found it hard to find the right words, but remember telling them that 'His life was not a bed of roses'. Finally, after five or six hours due to the many interruptions, I finished the obituary and filed it.

Here is part of it: 'In 1972 Bobby Fischer returned from Iceland to a hero's welcome in the U.S., but when he came back to Iceland late at night on the 24th of March in 2005, a warrant for his arrest had been issued in every state of the United States. Even when he was on his way back to Iceland from the Japanese detention centre where he had spent nine months, the U.S. embassy in Iceland informed a high ranked official within the Iceland foreign ministry that if Fischer would ever leave Iceland the U.S. authorities would have him arrested. In his autobiography soccer legend Pelé notes that at some point in his career his name started to take on a life of its own. The same applies for Bobby Fischer. His name towered over all the great players of chess history. On a global scale he transcended the game of chess.

'Bobby Fischer seems to have inspired many artists. Without ever appearing in the film himself, he is the main character in the movie *Searching for Bobby Fischer*. The musical *Chess* could never have been composed without Bobby Fischer. Why he rejected all the offers he had after the '72 match, I cannot explain. That he did not show up as World Champion in a match with Anatoly Karpov with a standing offer from the Philippines of 5 million U.S. dollars, was a fact difficult to accept.

'And the years went by. The papers wrote about Fischer's 'self-imposed exile' and a couple of times there were reports of a possible 'Fischer-match'. I met Boris Spassky in Seville, Spain, in the fall of 1987. He had just returned from Pasadena where he had met Fischer. He told me they had discussed a possible match. However, by that time attempts to get Bobby Fischer back to the chess board had for me become a rather tiring issue. Then in 1992 came his return match with Boris Spassky in Sveti Stefan and Belgrade. For his last victory Fischer had to pay a heavy price. By playing chess again, he was, according to U.S. officials, violating Executive

Order12810, signed by President George Bush in June of the same year. A warrant for his arrest was issued in the United States. Still, at the beginning of 1997, when his passport was about to expire, he managed to have it renewed in Bern, Switzerland. But in July 2004 he was arrested at Narita airport in Japan.

'He listened to music a lot, especially soul and blues. His favourite performer was Jackie Wilson. About ten years ago his mother passed away, and soon after his sister. He would never reveal much about his inner feelings, but often spoke his mind about any given matter, even if he knew that what he said didn't please the listener. Sometimes he went overboard in his statements. However, one must keep in mind that this usually happened when he was being confronted by what he felt was a great injustice. I am of the opinion that those who fought for his release from Japanese detention can be proud of their achievement. After all his only 'crime' had been to play chess. In Iceland he found shelter from the storm.'

After his death was announced there was a worldwide outpouring of articles on Bobby Fischer. Making a press statement in Moscow, Garry Kasparov remembered him in style: 'Fischer's beautiful chess and his immortal games will stand forever as a central pillar in the history of our game' was one of several noteworthy comments the former World Champion made.

One of the most startling contributions I read on the web was by a lady called Judy Winters from Port Charlotte in Florida, which still intrigues me today: 'Bobby Fischer was my first boyfriend. Starting about 1955, I would go to the Manhattan Chess Club with my father. My father would play and I would drink soda. I saw Bobby a few times there and we would talk a little. (We were both the same age and very shy) I fell in love with him at a tournament at Asbury Park, in New Jersey. We went to the boardwalk together, went on rides and played games of chance. His mother was real mad at him when we got back because he was almost late for his game.

'I think it was Memorial Day or Labour Day, maybe 1955 or 1958. The Asbury Park newspaper had a picture of me watching one of his games. I wish I could get a copy of that picture. We wrote back and forth for a while, and then I got too cool for chess and he got famous... I love remembering him in such an innocent time. He was just a person, like you and me, with a wonderful gift (and he was very cute). If anyone can get that picture from the Asbury Park newspaper, please let me know. I think it was on the front page, because we were only about 13 or 15, and he won.'

The following day, Saturday, January 19, the press started discussing possible funeral arrangements. The RJF Committee convened for a meeting at Gudmundur's house around noon. There were many unclear matters to be resolved. I had hoped that Gardar would be there, but it seemed he had now broken off all ties with the other members. Magnus Skulason was apparently not too eager to attend the meeting either. He did not want to come if Saemi would be present, because of the dispute about the documentary. Gudmundur had reassured him that there would only be himself, Einar and me.

I had been speaking to the president of the Icelandic Chess Federation, Gudfridur Lilja Gretarsdottir, and we decided to call her too. I had hoped to have as few people as possible involved in this, since we had obtained no approval from Miyoko regarding our involvement in the funeral arrangements because she was still in Japan. Gardar's absence of course complicated matters. I was hoping we could avoid the press, but when I arrived the first person I met was a young female reporter from Channel 2. Gudmundur told me she had called and he had decided to invite her over for a brief conversation.

At his home Gudmundur gave an interview to her and put forward a proposition which for a few days became a topic of heated debate. He proposed that Bobby's remains should be laid to rest at the national cemetery at Thingvellir. This idea did not sit well with the general public, and the media, especially DV, turned against the RJF Committee. The little church in the Thingvellir National Park in the south-west of Iceland occupies a significant place in the history of our country. According to Snorri Sturluson's history of the Norwegian kings, Heimskringla, the first church here was built back in 1015, when the Norwegian king Olaf the Portly sent over wood and a church bell. The present church was constructed in 1859, but two of the three bells are considerably older, as are other parts, such as the pulpit that dates back to 1683. In 1939 a small cemetery was consecrated behind the church. The only occupants of the Thingvellir cemetery are the Icelandic poets Jonas Hallgrimsson and Einar Benediktsson.

Jonas Hallgrimsson, who lived in the romantic era of the 19th century, was an artist of stellar magnitude, the best-loved poet who ever lived in Iceland. At the time of his death he was only 37 years old. His health had been deteriorating fast and over the years he had developed a severe alcohol problem. He died in Copenhagen in 1845. Returning from a night out he fell while climbing the stairs up to his room and broke his leg, which resulted in a severe and fatal infection. When he was buried only a few of his friends gathered around the grave, but everybody felt that Iceland had suffered a great loss. A hundred years later his remains were exhumed and brought to Iceland. This was a remarkable homecoming, as in his lifetime he was a bit of an outsider and not too well liked in the city of Reykjavik.

Einar Benediktsson was a failed businessman when he died, but a great poet. In 1930 the Althingi, the oldest parliament in the world, celebrated its 1,000th anniversary at Thingvellir. During the celebration Einar, then considered Iceland's national poet, was humiliated when he was not invited to a reception in honour of the Danish king Christian X. A decision that was clearly motivated by his alcoholism. At the time of his death in 1940 he was a recluse, who had lived the last few years of his life with his maid Hlin Johnson in a small cottage in Herdisarvik. This is close to the cliffs of Krisuvik, situated by the seaside close to Grindavik where Bobby stayed in a guesthouse for some time in the summer of 2007.

In their prime both Jonas Hallgrimsson and Einar Benediktsson were ignored by many of their own countrymen, so Gudmundur's suggestion that Bobby Fischer should be buried beside them was well worth considering. After all, one of the best-known tombstones in the Kremlin wall in Moscow is that of the American writer and fellow-traveller John Reed, the author of the classic on the Russian Revolution *Ten Days That Shook The World*.

The government was not attracted to the idea either. The Minister of Justice, Björn Bjarnason, took a firm stand against any such considerations on his website and Prime Minister Geir Haarde reacted with a silence that spoke volumes. Actually, within the previous cabinet David Oddsson had been the only one fighting for Bobby's release from Japan and his Icelandic citizenship. His colleagues at the time let him, but in fact they took no interest in the initiative.

On the evening of January 19 we still had not heard a word from Gardar. Finally he called me and we had a long conversation. It sounded as if he was not too eager to talk to me and one thing that he said stood out: 'It would be better for you not to know anything about Bobby's burial.'

It was clear that Gardar was planning something together with Miyoko and that no one was allowed to interfere. I contacted Einar Einarsson and another meeting was planned at his home the following day. A matter of concern had arisen, because we really wanted to have him buried in Iceland. As Miyoko was Buddhist, she might want to have Bobby cremated and perhaps take his ashes with her to Japan.

On Sunday, January 20, we called in a lawyer, Kristján Stefánsson, and he expressed the opinion that the RJF group was authorized to organize the burial. There was a consensus within the group that a meeting with Miyoko would clarify matters. I telephoned Gardar again and together with Magnus Skulason I went to see Gardar at his home. It was a very inconclusive meeting and in fact I failed to understand why he agreed to meet us at all. He told us that Miyoko would be bringing some valuable papers from Japan, such as their marriage certificate. From everything he said and did it seemed to be very important for Gardar to prevent those who had fought for Bobby's release to attend his funeral, even Magnus, who had spent long hours at Bobby's bedside in his last weeks.

That evening Miyoko's plane landed in Keflavik. Gardar picked her up and they drove to a 'secret location' south of Reykjavik, close to Selfoss, as we later found out. The next morning, on Monday, January 21, I phoned former Prime Minister David Oddsson to discuss the matter. He expressed his wish for Bobby's remains to be laid to rest on Icelandic soil. Around the same time I received a text message from Gardar, in which he stated that Miyoko was ready to meet members of the RJF group, but was unwilling to discuss the funeral.

A full explanation of what had been going on surfaced later that day when the Miyoko/Gardar plot hit the news. The Telegraph reported in the course of the week: '... the reclusive genius had arranged his own secret "guerrilla" burial. Now its legality is being questioned. The grave was dug in secret as darkness descended over the white frozen landscape around the village of Hraungerdi, ready for Bobby Fischer's last getaway. Not even the minister whose churchyard it was knew of the funeral planned for the following morning. Only five people attended the brief service early on Monday, conducted in the half-light before the short Icelandic day had properly begun. Among them was Gardar Sverrisson, Fischer's closest friend of the last few years and the man who had organised the digging of the grave without seeking the permission of Iceland's Lutheran Church or of the state authorities. Sverrisson had also secured the services of a Roman Catholic priest from Reykjavik, some 30 miles to the west. Fischer was not a Catholic but must have been content with the arrangement – Sverrisson would have followed the American's instructions to the letter. The fifth mourner may or may not have been Fischer's wife, a Japanese woman named Miyoko Watai. So much about Bobby Fischer was a mystery. He liked it that way, keeping people guessing. No way would the fallen angel of world chess have allowed the media a feeding frenzy. Hence the unauthorised "guerrilla" funeral uncovered by the Telegraph this week; a strange secret end to a strange secret life...

'The manner of his burial is now the subject of controversy in Iceland, an intimate society of just 300,000 people. Some of Fischer's friends believe the burial is unlawful. If Miss Watai was not his wife, they argue, then she and Sverrisson had no right to carry out the burial without seeking the permission of his estate's legal representatives. There is the additional matter of money: Fischer's Swiss bank account is thought to have held about £1.5 million, and there may be more in gold deposits.'

The cemetery where Bobby was buried was close to the house of Gardar's father-in-law. A crew from Channel 2 had gotten wind of the plans, but only arrived when the ceremony was over. A baffled audience was told by the reporter that Miyoko and Bobby had indeed been married but wanted to keep it a secret.

Were they married? While in the detention centre in Japan Bobby was getting desperate and the option to marry Miyoko in order to get out arose. Their attempt backfired and when Miyoko came to Iceland together with Bobby, she said in an interview they might try to tie the knot later as the Japanese authorities had blocked their attempts in 2004.

There is no doubt in my mind that Miyoko loved Bobby Fischer dearly. She came to Iceland every two to three months and would usually stay for about two weeks. Even though he mopped the floor, washed his dirty laundry and took good care of the things the owner had left, Bobby's flat at Klapparstigur was usually a bit messy when she arrived, with empty bottles of organic juices he had purchased scattered around the kitchen floor.

He always looked better when Miyoko was there with him, and he seemed happier. She brought order to his life, ironed his shirts, and bought new clothes for him, though strictly following his peculiar dress code. Sometimes she brought technical gadgets from Japan for him. Once he showed me a small but expensive radiation detector.

Bobby's daily attire consisted of jeans, sometimes a khaki shirt, and a light blue sweater. He constantly wore Birkenstock clogs, and then there were many sorts of caps. When Miyoko was with him I noticed he preferred a leather cap.

She had adjusted to all of his whims and sometimes even laughed when he talked about her poor chess playing skills. She was the only one with whom he still agreed to play the 'old chess'. 'The problem with Miyoko is that she is a terrible chess player', he once said, and we all laughed. But he admired her and respected her for a variety of reasons. 'You know, Helgi, Miyoko came to visit me in the detention centre every single day', he said. 'Travelling back and forth took her six hours every day.'

And although Bobby himself was completely alien to giving people presents, Miyoko would regularly send gifts such as perfumes, handkerchiefs or Japanese purses from Tokyo to my wife Sigurborg.

When I arranged an interview for *Morgunbladid* with Bobby in the summer of 2006 the subject of their marriage came up. Bobby's sole reason for agreeing to the interview was the conflict he had with the UBS bank in Switzerland, which had closed his bank account without his consent and transferred his money to Iceland. That was the only thing on his mind and that he wanted to talk about in the Three Fishes restaurant where we met. Apparently the journalist was more interested in his private life, but when he started to ask him 'Your wife Miyoko Watai...' Bobby stopped him short in his tracks by interrupting him. 'She is not my wife', he said in no uncertain terms. 'Oh, I mean your fiancée', the journalist corrected himself. 'She is not my fiancée. She is a friend', Bobby responded angrily.

I had driven Bobby to the interview but had some other obligations and decided to leave, as the journalist made it clear that he could give Bobby a lift back home. Later that day Bobby called and asked why I had left so early. He was far from happy with the journalist, who had shown him little respect. I told Bobby not to worry too much, the interview would come out fine. And it did. The UBS matter was part of it, but in the interview Bobby also expressed his admiration for Icelandic women, adding that almost everybody he had met had been nice to him.

After the funeral at Laugdælakirkja heated discussions began. I kept publicly silent and so did most of the other members of the RJF group. Bobby's brother-in-law Russell Targ arrived in Iceland for the funeral, but was surprised when he was told it had already taken place. From Bobby's viewpoint his family had ceased to exist long ago.

According to Gardar, Bobby wished to be buried in the small Catholic cemetery of Laugardaelir church, outside the small town of Selfoss. Bobby had been there with Gardar and his family a few times and allegedly he had said at one point that he could imagine finding his last resting place in this quiet surroundings. Did Bobby instruct Gardar that he wanted to be buried at Laugdælakirkja? For me this is hard to accept. Bobby was not prepared to die and it was not in his nature to plan anything of such importance ahead. You could not even order a table in a restaurant in advance.

Bobby was suffering from degenerative renal failure. At times I had noticed a vague smell of urine in his apartment in Klapparstigur. In October of 2007 it was obvious to everyone that something had to be done about his condition. Magnus and Gardar managed to talk him into visiting Landsspitalinn, carefully avoiding mentioning to him that this was in fact the top medical hospital in Iceland. His perception of Western medicine was far from positive, he had no trust in it at all. He stayed there from October until the middle of November and was released in somewhat improved condition. At the hospital the doctors gave him their cruel assessment of his physical deterioration several times. Nevertheless it was impossible to talk him into allowing any kind of surgery or even taking painkillers, although the nurses would use opium plasters whenever they could, which of course he was not aware of. If it were not so tragic it would have been funny, but as if to discourage the medical staff there was a book on his night desk on the subject of 'what doctors can do to you'. Boris Spassky wrote him a letter and asked him to listen carefully to what the doctors suggested. Fridrik Olafsson visited him frequently, but it is unlikely that he tried to persuade him to be treated, knowing his personality. Bobby suffered a lot.

In the summer of 2007 he had moved from the flat in Klapparstigur to a small flat at Espigerdi, in the eastern part of Reykjavik. When he returned there from Landsspitalinn, his condition continued to deteriorate. Miyoko arrived from Japan to spend Christmas with him, but when she left his condition worsened by the day. He was afraid to be alone and Magnus Skulason would come to Bobby's sparsely furnished flat on the 9th floor at Espigerdi 4 and stay with him for many long hours. With the help of Saemi, Bobby had purchased the flat in the summer of 2005. 'I just bought it as an investment', he told me. In the autumn of 2006 we tried to find a new entrance door, as he thought that the original door was too thin and weak to keep out any intruders. In the end Bobby got an offer for a specially imported German door, full of switches, locks and whatnot. The frame was probably thicker than the walls of the flat. The door cost approximately 10 thousand U.S. dollars, a price Bobby found rather steep, and in the end he kept the old door.

Within walking distance of his flat there was a bus stop from where he could go anywhere he wanted, but now he didn't go out anymore. Gardar and his wife were living on the 7th floor.

Gardar's wife was a nurse and she would also go and see him. Magnus would sometimes bring him freshly squeezed juices. One day he came in with a mixture of six juices in one big bottle. Bobby asked him which six fruits or vegetables were in it, but Magnus could not remember each and every sort put into this strange cocktail. Bobby looked at him in bewilderment and asked incredulously: 'How could you forget?' But he forgave him when Magnus explained to him that he had forgotten because of the enormous workload within the prison system of Iceland. As a psychiatrist he was dealing on a daily basis with the tragic cases of the inmates of a specially-built prison for those the legal system had deemed insane. He told Bobby that his memory was not as good as it used to be and on a few occasions it had failed him. Bobby was very considerate when he touched upon this topic. 'Has it been your sole purpose in life to help others?' he asked. Then he drank the juice Magnus brought him and he liked it.

Bobby was curious about the profession Magnus had chosen and asked him about the collaboration and later the breakup between Sigmund Freud and Carl Jung. He was thirsting for knowledge about their studies of dreams, telling Magnus that he was having the same dream over and over again. Magnus later regretted not having asked him about this dream.

Then came the last time Magnus was at Bobby's bedside in the early hours of January 15, 2008. 'I would speak in a monologue and he would fall asleep, like a baby', he told The Guardian. 'Then he would wake up with aches and pains and I would press some grapes and give him a glass of juice, or some goat's milk, which unfortunately he could not hold down. Once, towards dawn, he woke up and said his feet ached and asked if I could massage them. I tried my best, and it was then that he said his last words to me. Responding to my hands on his feet he said, with a terrible gentleness, "Nothing is as healing as the human touch."'

Because of the beauty of the expression, these words have often been quoted as Bobby's final words, but they were not. In the early morning of January 16 Dr. Eirikur Jonsson was with Bobby at his flat for his daily visit. At noon he decided to call for an ambulance and again Bobby, now terminally ill, was taken to Landsspitalinn. For the next 24 hours Eirikur and his staff took shifts at his bedside. At noon on Thursday the 17th Bobby Fischer passed away. Before he slipped into unconsciousness he was heard to whisper: 'I leave this to you.' Eirikur, when I asked him about these words, would neither deny nor confirm them.

Other matters that were not directly connected to his oath as a doctor he did talk about. 'Amid all the discussions about the human rights of patients, neither I nor any other doctor, and there were many who tried to persuade Bobby to accept proper treatment, had met a patient like Bobby Fischer', said Eirikur. 'At no time did his character leave him. For the doctors at Landspitalinn it was, simply put, a unique experience. A patient may object to a treatment or medication and doctors and medical staff at hospitals in Iceland respect their rights. In certain matters we may have to ask for their permission, for example to take a blood sample. We inform them about the risk involved if nothing is done, et cetera. When Bobby Fischer was admitted to Landspitalinn in October of 2007 we realized that this individual intended to fight his disease all by himself. That day in January his fight came to the only possible conclusion. It could not have been any other way. What an incredible fighter. But for me and so many others his death was a very traumatic experience.'

At the meeting at Gudmundur's home after Bobby's death, Magnus Skulason seemed emotionally devastated. He made a reference to the crucifixion of Christ and spoke bitterly about those who had betrayed Bobby. At such a moment, I assumed, every man has a right to find his own truth. I wanted to console him but was at a loss for words. But then silence is the eloquent expression of the inexpressible. Later, a friend who had heard about Bobby's last words from a reliable source, talked about his final moments and he also drew a parallel with Christ's crucifixion, more in particular the last words of Jesus, who is supposed to have said: 'Father, into your hands I commit my spirit.'

Such lofty thoughts were not on my mind. It was time for my own reflection. I thought back to our last conversation, when he had said, 'Don't listen to my negativity, Helgi.' And I thought about his rants, the infamous interviews and his stubborn anti-Semitism. For me they were the expression of a desperate soul. Rather than talking about issues that were seemingly in his heart, I believed that they were expressing his own inner feelings. To me it always seemed that he was just expressing how bad he felt.

I wasn't going to think of his negativity now. Not this time. I found myself thinking of the American chess players that I frequently played against in the seventies and eighties, players who all had been inspired by him. After the tournament in Lone Pine in 1977, I was travelling together by car with a couple of American players. I remember Junior World Champion Mark Diesen was there and so was Ron Henley. On our way we stopped for a few hours in Los Angeles in a house owned by a chess player by the name of Kim Commons. He had been a member of the U.S. team that won gold at the Haifa Olympiad of 1976. I noticed a book on his bookshelf that looked familiar. It was the collection of Bobby's games. When I opened it I saw that Kim Commons had written in it: 'All beauties.'

Chapter Sixteen

When suddenly Johnny gets the feeling he's being surrounded by
horses, horses, horses, horses
coming in in all directions.
Patti Smith, *Horses*

My last meeting with Bobby was on April 2, 2007. I had invited him to attend a big concert with various artists at NASA in downtown Reykjavik. He only wanted to see Björk perform. For most of the evening we sat on the second floor with Inga, the manager of NASA. She poured Bobby a few glasses of Bailey's on ice. I had never seen him drink this before, but I had read that this was what he was drinking on the plane from Japan. Bobby had seen Björk in Lars von Trier's film *Dancer in the Dark* and had been full of praise. After we had seen her show, Bobby was also enthusiastic about her music, saying, 'I immediately sensed her star quality.'

Funnily, on an earlier occasion I had brought up the issue of who was more famous, he or Björk. Bobby had little doubt. 'I am,' he said, 'long term.'

While we were sitting on the second floor a Chilean employee came upstairs and had a chat with Bobby. Because he was with me he assumed this bearded man was a chess player, but at first he had no idea that he was talking with Bobby Fischer. He asked Bobby whether he had been to South America and when he received an answer about several tournaments in Argentina it all of a sudden dawned on him whom he was talking to. Bobby spoke with him in fluent Spanish, just like he had spoken in Serbo-Croat with a Serbian waiter at a Mexican restaurant in 101 Reykjavik.

When the concert was over Bobby went downstairs with Inga to meet Björk. I didn't want to intrude and did not go along. They exchanged a few words and Bobby could not hide his admiration of soul music. When he reported on their meeting to me he said with a smile that Björk had stated: 'Soul is dead.' He took it as a joke and didn't mind. He was in an excellent mood and it was clear that he was very fond of her.

I spoke with Bobby Fischer almost every day for a long period of time, but we also communicated on another level. Having made a thorough study of Bobby's career, there was hardly a position from his games I did not know something about. He was surprised how accurate I was about certain dates.

'You have an astonishing memory', he once said. 'No, it's nothing special. I am just like everybody else', I said. 'No, no. It's a special talent', he insisted. I then pointed at a book about Nasser, the former president of Egypt, that Bobby had recently purchased. It was lying on top of a stack of books in his living room. 'Do you remember where you were when Nasser died?' I asked. 'Yes. I was in Siegen', Bobby answered, almost surprised. Then he looked at me and smiled.

Bobby was fascinated by famous people and among his favourite books were biographies of statesmen and historical figures. But he also followed the celebrities of today. One evening when we were dining in The Players, a sports bar in Kopavogur, I asked him: 'What do you think of Tiger Woods?' I was watching a golf tournament on the PGA tour and Bobby seemed not very interested. He had told me before that he never liked golf and especially mentioned 'the stupid-looking trousers' golfers wore.

'I think he is ugly', Bobby said.

'No, c'mon Bobby, he looks great', I countered.

'Do they play in those tournaments every week?' he then asked. I didn't reply immediately. Tiger was on the green trying to sink a long putt for a birdie. I waited and he had a near miss and then I said: 'Yes, they play every week. But Tiger can afford to take a break more often than the other players.'

The name Tiger Woods had popped up in our conversation before. In the spring of 2005, a column appeared in *Time* magazine, written by Charles Krauthammer, entitled: 'Did chess make him crazy?'

'Bobby Fischer is back in Iceland, and that is as it should be. Fischer put Iceland on the map for the first time since the Vikings happened by. And Iceland put Fischer on the map, providing the venue for his greatest triumph, the 1972 world chess championship. That was before he fell off a psychic cliff. No one is too upset about this arrangement because he's clearly a sick man. His insane rants about Jews and America, his choice of a squalid, furtive life by a man who could have lived in princely admiration, his paranoia – he had the fillings in his teeth removed because if "somebody took a filling out and put in an electronic device, he could influence your thinking" – evoke pity and puzzlement.

'Fischer is the poster boy for the mad chess genius... Plausible, perhaps, but there are lots of folks who are monomaniacal in other "trivial" spheres and who come out psychically intact. Tiger Woods was raised from infancy to be a great golfer and is not just intact but graceful and charming.'

Speaking to Bobby on the phone I told him about the column. 'It's a very unpleasant article', I said, suggesting that perhaps he better not read it. 'It does not bother me one bit,' Bobby answered, 'it is all manipulated stuff by the editors and publishers of *Time* and Warner Brothers.'

At Players there were several snooker and pool tables in a nearby room on the same floor. After dinner we watched the quiet action in there and at some point I suggested a game. He agreed. As it turned out Bobby was a far better player than me. I asked him where he had learned to play so well, a question that led to an unexpected argument. 'Well, I played quite a bit during the Stockholm Interzonal in 1962', he answered. He added that his main playing partner at the snooker table had been Miguel Cuellar from Colombia. About their game at the Interzonal he said: 'I beat him there with an early b5.'

'No, no, that's wrong,' I immediately said, 'you are confusing the game with the one you played against him at the Sousse Interzonal.'

Bobby did not give in. He did not seem to remember the Sousse game too well. Later I found out that we had both been right. He had indeed played Cuellar in both Interzonals and in both games as Black he played an early b5.

Having discovered his skills at the snooker table I phoned a golfing partner of mine, Gunnar Örn Hreidarsson, who also happens to be one of the best snooker players in Iceland. I asked him to spend some time with Bobby and play a little. We agreed to meet at Lagmuli, a street in the eastern part of Reykjavik where they had an enormous snooker room. As we walked in, Bobby said that it reminded him of New York. Before Gunnar arrived, Bobby took out his pocket chess set. We sat down and analysed a position from the 24th game of the first Karpov-Kasparov match. When Gunnar came in he helped Bobby with his pose and his grip on the cue. They played and out of ten frames Bobby won twice. It was fun to watch his fighting spirit because he was playing this game without the burden of having to prove anything. When they parted they decided to play some other time. Gunnar told me that Bobby called him a few times afterwards, but they failed to schedule another meeting.

After Bobby's death people often asked me if I considered him a friend. Once he said to me, almost with the honesty of an innocent child: 'I am a difficult person.' There was no denying that. Still, the answer I gave came quite naturally: 'Yes, I did.'

131

Asked for a comment in Wijk aan Zee the day after Bobby's death, Lajos Portisch explained that friendship with Bobby Fischer was always difficult.

'He never became anybody's friend. He never gave, only accepted', Fridrik Olafsson said in an interview with New In Chess.

When Bobby returned to Iceland in 2005 he found in Saemi Palsson a friend and an invaluable aid. Saemi brought along his keen understanding of Bobby's character, invited him for dinner at his home on several occasions, drove him around, swam with him, helped him find a lawyer and took care of many practical matters. Bobby called him 'street smart'. Just like Saemi, Bobby was a very good swimmer, and back in 1972 they would even compete. But he very much disliked the chlorine in the swimming pools. 'The Jews put chlorine in the swimming pools to destroy your eyes', he insisted. The swimming pool at Seltjarnarnes, close to Saemi's house, mainly has sea water in it and Bobby did go there hesitantly a few times. He also went to the Blue Lagoon geothermal spa.

In the summer of 2005 Saemi was hospitalized. Bobby visited him frequently and was very considerate towards Saemi's physical discomfort. I visited Saemi once and Bobby was there when I entered the hospital room. Bobby probably did not get the best possible upbringing, but his hardworking single mother Regina must be given credit for one thing: from an early age she would let Bobby visit the sick.

Still, in the 33 years that separated 2005 from 1972 Bobby and Saemi had drifted apart. His return was humiliating, of course, compared to the dawn of July 4, 1972, an arrival that I regard as one of the most dramatic ever witnessed in the history of any competition.

That Tuesday morning Bobby was taken in an escorted car to a house on the outskirts of Reykjavik and Saemi the policeman was put on guard in front of the house. That's where they met for the first time. Saemi was later hired as Bobby's bodyguard. Bobby would stay at his house many times during the match and on at least one occasion he babysat for Saemi and his wife.

When Bobby returned triumphantly to the U.S. in September 1972, he asked Saemi to come along. He stayed with Bobby in California for three months. He clearly filled the gap Ed Edmondson had left. In the years that they didn't see each other, Bobby distanced himself from chess and educated himself, even if many of the books he was devouring were rather one-dimensional. Still, their relations remained the same and again Saemi became Bobby's humble servant, taking all sorts of humiliations from his temperamental master.

For some it was difficult to fathom why anyone could tolerate such a person, given his outbursts, his racist comments and all. As for me, I simply did not allow him to express his anti-Semitic views. Whenever he was about to start his rants, I put up a wry face and made it clear I was not going to listen. 'What is this? What face is this?' he would say, seemingly irritated by my total lack of interest in his favourite subject.

Sometimes, waiting for him in his flat when he was getting ready to go out, I hummed a tune. I don't know why I did this and once Bobby looked at me and said: 'I think I know your philosophy. It's like in the Monty Python song. Life's a bowl of shit no matter what you make of it. Look on the bright side of life. Am I right?' I kept quiet.

During one of my visits he was once again absorbed by the issue of 'the Jews'. He had opened an old book on the Holocaust. There was a photo of families waiting for a train which would ultimately take them to their deaths in the concentration camps. 'You know, Helgi,' he said, 'the Germans took everything from these people. And it was all illegal. But when the Jews stole everything from me it was all legal.'

I sat down by the kitchen table. 'I know you have been robbed, Bobby.' When he missed a payment on his monthly bill, Bekins Storage auctioned off his memorabilia. Among the many things he had in the storage room there was a chess set John Lennon and Yoko Ono had sent him after the match in '72. Bobby had collected many valuable things during his career.

But there was no way to talk him out of his idée fixe about the Jews. I tried, hoping that his many years with the Worldwide Church of God, founded by Herbert W. Armstrong, and his studies of Christianity would help. I suggested that he should forgive his enemies: 'It is always helpful. It works. It's the fundament of Christianity', I said. 'But that's what the Jews want. They want you to forgive them, so they can carry on robbing you', Bobby answered. However, another day Bobby would tell me: 'You know, Helgi, I am a very forgiving person.'

The stacks of books Bobby had in his flat dealt with many historically important issues, especially before and during the Second World War. For some reason our conversation once touched on the making of the nuclear bomb. I told him that not only could I lend him the book J. Robert Oppenheimer: Shatterer of Worlds, but also the entire transcript of the hearings before the Personnel Security Board in 1954. Most of it, approximately 1,000 pages, was in small letters, but Bobby told me he liked such detailed books.

In his flat the BBC was turned on for more than ten hours a day. But despite all his reading and listening to the radio, there was an emptiness in Bobby's existence. He was not playing chess and the work on the clock had been laid to rest. He had to find ways to spend his time. Normally he would go out late in the afternoon. He preferred to dine at the vegetarian restaurant A Naestu Grösum on the shopping street Laugavegur or at some of the Thai restaurants in Reykjavik. Another of his favourites was 3 Frakkar, where according to the owner Ulfar Eysteinsson his favourite was catfish. Sometimes he would prepare a meal himself. I recall him telling me once over the phone that he was cooking some pasta.

He regularly paid Bragi a visit at his Bokin bookshop. He had his own chair, where he would read and sometimes doze off, and occasionally he would help Bragi stack the books. He liked the bookshop because it reminded him of New York in the old days. When I asked him where he got hold of all his old books and Russian chess magazines when he was young, he mentioned a bookshop in Manhattan.

Bragi and his son Atli, who ran the bookshop, noticed that Bobby developed an interest in books written by 'outlaws'. He asked me whether I had read Oscar Wilde's *The Picture of Dorian Gray* as we were driving around Reykjavik one very windy day and he looked out the window of the car at the high waves of the Atlantic Ocean. 'This is raw', he said.

Bobby would never acknowledge if he was going through a tough period. Most people who had gone through what he had been through in the nine months he spent in the Japanese detention centre would be in need of counselling. Sometimes he was very bitter, cynical and disillusioned. Nevertheless, after he settled in Iceland I never heard him repeat the wicked things he had said in the radio interviews during his stay in Hungary and Japan. It is a real tragedy how he disgraced himself time and again in those radio interviews.

I told him at our first meeting that such statements were unacceptable. About the 9/11 interview he later simply told me: 'I was tricked.' Bobby was not in a stable condition when Eugenio Torre and the journalists from the Filipino radio station phoned him after the attacks on the Twin Towers. They knew what to expect from him.

Before Bobby's last radio interview, at Saga Radio in the autumn of 2006, I pleaded with him to be careful with his choice of words. 'Bobby, please try to tone down some of your views', I urged him. Bobby was silent for a while, but then he said: 'Look, Helgi, no one will interfere with my views about anything.' But in the interview Bobby saved us all from embarrassment. It came out fine. It may have had something to do with the host, Sigurdur Tomasson, who did an excellent job. The controlled voice of Bobby in this interview may be attributed to the fact that Icelanders in general have little or no interest in racial debates and he had noticed that his political opinions were almost a laughing matter in Iceland. For chess fans it was interesting to hear him describe his early days at the Manhattan Chess Club and give his impressions of the great masters of the past:

'Morphy and Capablanca had enormous talent, Steinitz was very great too. Alekhine was great, but I am not a big fan of his. Maybe it's just my taste. I've studied his games a lot, but I much prefer Capablanca and Morphy. Alekhine had a rather heavy style, Capablanca was much more brilliant and talented, he had a real light touch. Everyone I've spoken to who saw Capablanca play still speaks of him with awe. If you showed him any position he would instantly tell you the right move. When I used to go to the Manhattan Chess Club back in the fifties, I met a lot of old-timers there who knew Capablanca, because he used to come around to the Manhattan club in the forties – before he died in the early forties. They spoke about Capablanca with awe. I have never seen people speak about any chess player like that, before or since. Capablanca really was fantastic. But even he had his weaknesses, especially when you play over his games with his notes, he would make idiotic statements like, "I played the rest of the game perfectly." But then you play through the moves and it is not true at all. But the thing that was great about Capablanca was that he really spoke his mind, he said what he believed was true, he said what he felt.'

When Bill Hook's memoir *Hooked on Chess* was published and there was an interview with the author in *New In Chess*, I told Bobby about the stories Hook told about the Flea House, the legendary chess club on 42nd street in New York. 'That place had flavour', Bobby said.

What kind of person was he? A man of primitive emotions, perhaps. On his arrival I was worried that he would never assimilate into Icelandic society. He learned a few words in Icelandic. I taught him the name of the mountain facing him every morning. 'Esja,' he would repeat after me, 'it reminds me of Grouse Mountain in Vancouver.' He could be kind to kids, cats, and other animals. He liked small kids and he embraced them, this was nice to watch.

He both liked and disliked attention. In the midst of groups he was a lonely man. Every time he walked the streets of Reykjavik his presence attracted attention. At first he did not seem to mind too much. Later he usually left his flat after dark. Sometimes he would take a nap in strange places like the cinema, libraries or Bragi's bookshop. When I went with him to see the Spielberg film Munich he was asleep during an episode where the main character is living in Brooklyn. He woke up just before the film ended and he did not want to leave the theatre immediately because he wanted to read the credits. 'I am sure some of the scenes were shot in Budapest', he said. And he was right about that.

In the book Fischer vs. Spassky that he wrote together with Fridrik Olafsson about the match in '72, Freysteinn Johannsson states that in the U.S. people were concerned about Bobby's security after the terrorist attack at the 1972 Munich Olympics and that precautionary measures were taken by the U.S. embassy in Reykjavik to ensure his safety. I asked Bobby about this matter and he told me that nothing of that sort happened.

Bobby was curious about people's professions, asking them perceptive questions about their work. The incredible and newfound wealth of some Icelanders amazed him. He coldly rejected the possibility that the boom could have a sound basis: 'You are living on borrowed time', he would say, adding that the privatization of the Icelandic banks was a big mistake. How right he was.

And he enjoyed chatting with nearly anybody. Once he took the street bus to Breidholt. There was a group of young boys on the bus and they decided to sit down beside him and start talking with him. He told me he liked the conversation.

What was utterly disturbing about him, however, was when for no apparent reason he would transform, becoming rude or even hostile. And he seemed to detest nearly all organizations, the Freemasons topping the list. Unfortunately, Saemi was 'a Mason', and that was one of the accusations Bobby launched at him when they fell out about the documentary film.

In his introduction of the players in the book on the second Piatigorsky Cup in Santa Monica in 1966, the sponsor Gregor Piatigorsky writes about Bobby: 'Tense and taciturn, one felt there was something tormenting deep down in him that he would not reveal.' And then he adds a comment by a friend of his: 'Fischer is a volcano which only chess can make rumble and erupt – without chess it would be extinct.'

The psychiatrist Magnus Skulason was of the opinion that he never really overcame the split with his mother, having to start living alone in her Brooklyn flat at age 16. 'I don't like people in my hair', he famously declared, referring to their strained relationship.

'Life goes on but the thrill of living is gone', he replied to my 'How's life?' question somewhere in the early months of 2007. I believe that Bobby Fischer was suffering from depression. Taking medication or seeing a psychiatrist was never an option for him. He lay in bed for a good part of the day, a common sign of a depressive mood. And the constant nostalgia was in his case just another form of depression. Many times when I visited him and he opened the door only after the customary question 'Who is it?' – even though as always I had already informed him about my arrival at the doorbell downstairs – he was still wearing his underwear or pyjamas, indicating that he had not been out of bed the whole day.

When I brought a technician from Siminn, the largest telephone company in Iceland, to fix his computer, he let us in and then hid away in his bedroom. He even called me on his mobile from the bedroom, asking how the work was progressing.

About his fight with the Swiss UBS bank he said to me, 'It was a godsend.' Which to my mind meant that now he had something to work on and give his energy to. The lawyers who looked into the matter were surprised that Bobby flatly dismissed any suggestions of striking a deal with UBS. He was at war with the bank, a war he intended to win. For him winning against a bank meant that UBS would lose some customers, and he especially mentioned Iran.

Tragically, all his adult years Bobby was preoccupied by materialistic considerations. Paradoxically he refused all business deals when the brand name Bobby Fischer carried value. The book *Bobby Fischer Teaches Chess* sold over a million copies. They say Elvis Presley buried jewellery in the garden of Graceland. Their insecurity was formed in early childhood and in the case of Bobby Fischer it never left him.

'I am only interested in money, women and the Jewish conspiracy', he said to me late at night as we sat in a small restaurant close to the Hotel Loftleidir shortly after he had arrived in Reykjavik. I tried to point out that with his modest lifestyle and all his money in a Swiss bank he could lead a very good life living only on the interest rates. But he insisted that in spite of money in the bank he considered himself as poor as any man could be, considering his fame and accomplishments.

But then we changed the subject. Our conversation brought us back to America. We discussed the war in Vietnam. I became excited about the miserable role Robert McNamara, the Secretary of State for Presidents John F. Kennedy and Lyndon B. Johnson, had played in the Vietnam War.

'You know, I once met McNamara in L.A.', he said. 'I think it was in 1968. I was looking at a beautiful car when the owner arrived and opened the door and asked me what I was doing. 'Nothing special. Just looking at the car. Fine piece of equipment', I told him. He looked at me and I had a distinct feeling that he knew me.' 'Then at a reception in Manila held by President Marcos and his wife Imelda in 1973, I met McNamara there', Bobby added.

Bobby Fischer was from the baby-boomer generation, but it seemed his path never crossed with any of the radical members of his generation, be they beatniks, the rock and roll generation, hippies or anyone involved in the happenings of the sixties. In that respect he was somewhat out of touch. The music of the Beatles came up one evening when we were dining at a restaurant called Jarlinn in downtown Reykjavik. Bobby liked their music, but preferred their earlier efforts from 1961 to '65.

He had not heard of rock singer Patti Smith when in August of 2005 I was asked to arrange a meeting between the two of them. A concert promoter called me and said that at the top of her wish list during her stay in Iceland, which was part of a European tour, was a meeting with Bobby Fischer. Just weeks before she came to Reykjavik she had been in Paris, where she was made Commander of the *Ordre des Arts et des Lettres* by the French Ministry of Culture.

They met in the restaurant at the Hotel Borg, the hotel Bobby had stayed in during his first visit to Iceland in 1960. Bobby didn't have the faintest idea that he was meeting the grandmother of punk. I was not quite sure what was expected of me. Hotel Borg was within walking distance of Bobby's home on Klapparstigur. I told Bobby that I intended to leave and either he could walk home or he could also give me a call later and I would drive him home. 'Oh, please stay', Patti said to me. And I did. I would have liked to discuss two of her 'favourite lads' with her, Arthur Rimbaud and Jim Morrison, but she took me for a bodyguard and that was all right.

On Artblog, one Matthew Langley later wrote:

'This surprised me most. I'm a chess guy (not hardcore – I don't read about openings and stuff) and never would I have thought Patti would have brought up Bobby Fischer. We were talking about people she had met and he came up kind of randomly – they met toward the end of his life in Iceland. There were serious rules about this meeting as well – only one bodyguard for each of them – Patti laughs – I don't have a bodyguard – so I brought along a member of the crew. Fischer was crazy about Rock 'n Roll,

Patti says that he told her one of the main reasons that he would play at Washington Square Park was so that he could get money to go see music in the evening – he loved the Four Tops and the Temptations.'

'I think I have my place in music history', Patti Smith told Bobby when he inquired about her career in music. She told him that she had been working in a large bookshop in 1966 when the publisher threw a party there when *Bobby Fischer Teaches Chess* hit the market. Bobby and Patti spoke for two hours. Their conversation was cordial and Bobby was very gentlemanly. I think he made a favourable impression on her. Slightly surprisingly she said at some point, 'I somehow always knew you were into music.' She promised to send him some of her works, and I believe she did. When they parted Bobby expressed his happiness about finally meeting someone from his home country.

Somewhere in the autumn of 2005, when we were sitting in a small restaurant close to Fossvogur and a beach by the name of Nautholsvik, our conversation once again brought us to New York City.

'I once saw Joe Louis on the streets of Manhattan', Bobby said. 'He was a mountain of a man. You know, they hired him at a big hotel in Las Vegas. Just to shake hands with the visitors and guests.' But now it was closing time. We were the only people left. The waiter, a beautiful woman in her early twenties, came over and politely informed us that she had to close the place.

Epilogue

After his death the fight over Bobby's estate was initially between Miyoko Watai and Bobby's nephews Alexander and Nicholas Targ, the children of his sister Joan and Russell Targ. For a long time not much was heard from the third party involved. In late November of 2009 Marilyn Young, Bobby's live-in partner in the Philippines, and her daughter Jinky travelled to Iceland together with lawyer Samuel Estimo and Bobby's friend and second during the 1992 match with Spassky, the Filipino grandmaster Eugenio Torre.

This was Marilyn and Jinky's second visit to Iceland in a span of four years. The only time Bobby mentioned Jinky to me was on a day when I went to see him and he noted that she was born on almost the same date as my oldest son, who was with me. My son was born on May 17, 2001, and she was said to have been born on May 21 of the same year. But he didn't call her his daughter. It was also clear to me that he was looking for an apartment for Marilyn and Jinky in Reykjavik, but even during our searches he didn't tell me explicitly that it was for them. I didn't ask him personal questions and anything he said about his private life was brought up by himself, but during our fishing trip with Big Joe and Viggo there was a moment when I suddenly asked him if Jinky was his daughter. Or rather, I suggested that she was his daughter to challenge him. He didn't give an answer. He only said: 'Why do people always want to know about my private life?' And that was it. Still, from what I have heard hardly a day went by after Marilyn and Jinky parted with Bobby in the autumn of 2005 that he would not call them.

On December 1 Marilyn, Jinky, Estimo and Torre, together with the Philippine consul in Iceland, Maria Priscilla Zanoria, visited Bobby's grave in the small cemetery in front of Laugadaelir church in Selfoss. Before they arrived their Icelandic lawyer Thordur Bogason had filed the estate claim. Marilyn and Jinky had their blood samples taken for DNA testing at Landsspitalinn, the same hospital Bobby had been rushed to on January 16, 2008. Marilyn gave an interview to RUV, the Icelandic state television. 'A woman always knows', she said when asked about the paternity of her daughter. 'Bobby will turn in his grave if the inheritance of his daughter will not be awarded', Eugenio Torre was quoted as saying.

At first the District Court of Reykjavik turned down Marilyn's request to have Bobby Fischer exhumed as no biological sample of him could be found. The Supreme Court of Iceland overturned the ruling, accepting the argument put forward by Jinky's lawyer that she had the right to know if Bobby Fischer was her real father. Additional evidence, such as postcards from Bobby to Marilyn and Jinky, and money sent by him to support them, played a role in the Supreme Court's decision.

On the Sunday night of July 5, 2010, on the orders of the Icelandic Supreme Court, the remains of Bobby Fischer were exhumed. The exhumation was conducted under a tent and the coffin was not unearthed or moved in any manner. A hole was dug in the side of the grave and from there they drilled into the coffin to extract a tissue sample. Present were the pastor of Selfoss, Kristinn Agust Fridfinnsson, members of the local parish, a doctor and medical staff, Olafur Helgi Kjartansson, the sheriff in Selfoss, and several other law enforcement representatives.

The results of the DNA tests were submitted to Reykjavik's District Court that August. Afterwards Thordur Bogason, Marilyn and Jinky's Icelandic lawyer made a public statement saying that the report excluded Bobby Fischer from being the father of Jinky Young.

In early March 2011 Reykjavik's District Court determined that Miyoko Watai had indeed been married to Bobby Fischer. As a consequence she is the sole heir of Bobby Fischer. The verdict was based on Miyoko's marriage document dated September 6, 2004, that was submitted to the court. Fischer's nephews Alexander and Nicholas Targ in turn appealed to the Icelandic Supreme Court. The final verdict in this dispute was given on April 8, 2011. The Supreme Court decided that Miyoko and Bobby were married in spite of Bobby's 'absent' passport. Fischer's nephews were, however, freed from shouldering the considerable costs of the trials, which according to my information amounted to approximately $100,000.

Since his death several more books have been written about Bobby. Also new films have appeared, the HBO documentary by Liz Garbus, *Bobby Fischer Against the World*, and the Icelandic documentary, *Me and Bobby Fischer*. One aspect which is often ignored in the attention paid to Bobby is his style of play, his approach to the game at the board. Sitting in Laugardalsholl in 1972 and watching Bobby Fischer was simply a wonderful experience. Today the game has advanced and evolved, not least because of the role of the computer. Even Bobby Fischer's finest wins barely hold up in comparison with the exploits of Garry Kasparov or some of today's top grandmasters. Still, he beats every other World Champion in at least one category. At the chessboard his all-important asset was his tremendous fighting spirit and concentration. Even Kasparov admitted that he did not have it. Of today's top players Veselin Topalov has declared that Bobby Fischer was his model: never agree to a draw or offer a draw yourself; don't walk around the stage like the Russians, but sit through the game and fight it out. The current number one in the world rankings, Norwegian grandmaster Magnus Carlsen, seems to possess the same fighting spirit.

A few years ago I met Argentinian grandmaster Miguel Quinteros, Bobby's old friend, who played an interesting game with him at the Buenos Aires tournament in 1970 and who was in Reykjavik in 1972 for a good part of the match. Our conversation naturally turned to Bobby and we concluded that we had to be grateful for having met him, even though he was a 'difficult person', as Bobby would readily acknowledge.

Acknowledgements

First of all I want to thank Dirk Jan ten Geuzendam, the editor of *New In Chess*, for giving me the opportunity to write about Bobby Fischer the way I saw him. We discussed the possibility of writing this book back in 2006, during the Chess Olympiad in Turin, Italy. Then in January 2008, when Dirk Jan came to Reykjavik, the final decision about the book was made.

At first Dirk Jan brought to my assistance an energetic woman, Sarah Hurst, who read through the text, corrected many things and made many interesting suggestions. I am indebted to her for the many Skype sessions we had in the summer of 2010.

Bragi Halldorsson and Stefan Baldursson read the text at various stages and so did my wife and best friend Sigurborg.

While preparing the text for print Dirk Jan diligently went through everything and for his involvement I am truly grateful. Needless to say, any error, factual or otherwise, is my sole responsibility.

Special thanks to Einar Einarsson for his photos that were published in this book. About the other guys who joined us on the mission to get Bobby Fischer out of the Japanese detention centre, Gudmundur G. Thorarinsson, Magnus Skulason, Ingvar Asmundsson, Gardar Sverrisson and Saemundur Palsson, it is fair to say that at times we had our differences, but it was all worthwhile.

Finally, I want to thank Bobby for all the beautiful games, the time we spent together and all the excitement. I am 'pretty sure' he never intended to change my life, but he did.